CAME THE DARK HORSE

CAME THE DARK HORSE

Horseracing Stories For Horseracing Fans

PATRICK LAWRENCE GILLIGAN

Published by Random Horse Publications

ISBN Hardcover: 978-1-7328892-8-6

Printed in the United States of America

Front Cover Artwork: Jacqueline Stanhope. Rushcutter Bay.
Back Cover Photo: Cheryl McEntee
Cover and Interior Design: Creative Publishing Book Design

For Chris Smith who supported me,
encouraged me and edited me.

Contents

Introduction

I am a Thoroughbred, the most beautiful of the noblest of beasts. I have been bred for my power and speed and men compete and bid millions to own the finest of us.

We do not take others flesh, our ancestors grazed on verdant plains.

But we are warriors, gladiators. So we are stabled and trained and honed and perfected. We become strong, we become fit, we are bathed and groomed and fed and the finest doctors attend to us. Our shoes are new each month, even when those who serve us have holes in theirs.

When we race, people gather, crowds of people flock. They come to watch us as we walk in the paddock, our necks arched our eyes liquid our bodies taut and naked and shining.

Then the riders emerge wearing dazzling colors of silk and they are raised onto our backs and I shall carry mine with some care, but I am alive now, I know the battle is upon us, so the rider must be sharp, his balance must be good and his muscles must be strong to manage me.

We step out upon the track and instantly I coil, my haunches lower and then I push forward, my quarters have the strength of a dozen men I carry my rider effortlessly as we warm up on the track alone in our world, just the gladiators and their riders.

I walk into the gate, I can see the track in front of me through the grills. My rider wears his goggles now, maybe six pairs, to be stripped off one by one through the race as the flying dirt clouds them. I have no goggles, the dirt shall hit my face, sting my eyes, enter my nostrils enter my throat, afterwards my eyes shall be sore, I shall be coughing, my lungs will be burning. But I accept all that because I am gladiator.

I have been bred for 400 years, my ancestors roamed deserts with the ancient Bedouins. Our names and prowess recorded all that time. So I take on my challenge, I ignore the pain my legs feel, my lungs feel, as we close to that winning post. My heritage gives me pride, it is bred into me. It is what I was born to be.

Now we are running, it is all noise, the riders growl and shout, their sticks strike our shoulders. Each stride we push forward into the air, momentarily floating above the ground, stride after stride, too quick to see. No-one knew we could fly until the moving camera was invented and then people were amazed.

We turn into the straight and then when the roar of the crowd comes upon us, the riders raise their whips and bring them down upon us, the strikes raise us further, we run harder to the winner's post.

And then it is done, we gallop out in silence to the backstretch, slowing, regaining our breath. Maybe a pat from the rider for the winner. We return to our carers. They may be happy, they may be disappointed, they may be angry, sometimes if we are hurt they may be sad. We have no say in their emotions, we have all fought hard, we tried our best, that is all we can do.

Race after race, battle after battle. Until, eventually it is decided I have fought enough. And then, through age or injury, then I am retired and if I am lucky I shall get to graze those verdant plains as my ancestors did and someone may love me just for who I am, not for what I can do for them.

If I am not lucky though, I could suffer a terrible fate. My last days, hours, minutes or seconds an unthinkable nightmare of terror. It is not in my power to decide. That is the fate of the gladiators. The thumb may be up, or it may be pointed down.

What follows are some stories of some of us, and some stories of those of you who chose to spend some time with us.

CHAPTER 1

The Korea Cup Part I

When I went to see Kenny McPeek in late December 2017 about taking a position as his assistant, he fed me a line about how he would like to take more horses to race in the UK, target some big races there, maybe even base some horses there at times. I spent many years training in the UK, in Newmarket. My son was born and raised there. That appealed to me. I took the job. He sent me to Saratoga for the summer. He sent me to Florida for the winter. He sent me to Canada. This morning I woke up in South Korea.

South Korea lies nearly 7,000 miles west of Kentucky. Seoul, its capital, is situated in the north west of the country, it is a progressive, advanced city of 10 million people, in a country of 50 million. Japan is an hour's flight east, and China an hour's flight west. It would be hard to find somewhere further from the UK to send me. I don't know if Kenny is trying to tell me something.

I am pleased to be here though. I am here because we are running Harvey Wallbanger in the Keeneland Korea Cup. And Kenny gave my son Jack Gilligan the ride.

Harvey Wallbanger was in Kenny's barn at Keeneland Race Course the day I started. A handsome 2-year old colt by Congrats, still learning the basics. A nice character who would come out of his stall each morning like an overexcited school kid let out of the classroom. I was in Saratoga with him for his debut. He finished second, I lost money. The horse who beat him ('TDN Rising Star'Complexity, by Maclean's Music) won a Grade I at Belmont next time. His second start was at Keeneland, he was beaten a nose. I lost money on him. The horse who beat him (Plus Que Parfait, by Point of Entry) went on to win the G2 UAE Derby.

When I decided to stop betting Harvey Wallbanger, Harvey Wallbanger decided to start winning. He won his maiden at Churchill, then he won the GII Fasig-Tipton Holy Bull S. at Gulfstream Park in the New Year. Things didn't really work out after that. He was given some time off and came back and ran a solid fourth in the Ellis Park Derby last month. If the race has brought him along, then we could be in business.

The fledgling Keeneland Korea Cup, just a 4-year-old race has this year been given Grade 1-Korean status (as Korea is a Part II country, it is simply black- type internationally) due to the presence of high-quality Japanese runners that have regularly farmed the approximately $800,000 contest. There are no Japanese runners this year though. Korea and Japan are engaged in a trade spat, that has evolved into a trade war, that has evolved into a diplomatic crisis, which means the Korea Racing Authority was unable this year to invite any Japanese-based contenders. This opens the race up and makes challengers from

North America and Europe the favourites to take the contest this year. It is an ill trade wind that blows no one any good.

The Korea Racing Authority is progressive and ambitious, it has two main racetracks, and a crowd of 30,000 per race day is typical. The Seoul Racecourse can hold 80,000 spectators, and come Sunday it will be about full for South Korea's biggest races (from a monetary perspective, in any event). The KRA already boasts the seventh biggest horserace betting turnover in the world, and it looks like that figure is set to keep climbing.

They had the funds then, to look after the invited connections, so upper business class tickets were complementary. Knowing I was facing a 14- hour flight to Seoul, I suggested to Kenny that it might be a good idea if I took his ticket as he wouldn't be attending. He said fine, but that it was really not that big a deal compared to a standard ticket.

He could not have been more wrong. I enjoyed the champagne, polished off my filet steak, watched a movie while sipping a couple of vodkas, then pressed the button that turned my seat into a bed, pulled the duvet over me, and rested my head on the pillow in my private cubicle. I woke up when the captain announced we were 20 minutes from landing.

That is as far from a standard flight as it is possible to get. To be sandwiched in a narrow upright seat with no legroom next to some flatulent old man who spends the entire journey muttering to himself is not a pleasant experience (that's what Jack tells me anyway). When you are relaxing in that cubicle you feel like one of life's winners, like you are a chosen one. You really are special–in a good way! When you are flying in economy on a long-haul flight, it gives you a lot of time to reflect on the fact that, let's face it, all your dreams didn't really work out.

So, if you want your kids to really shine and do well in life, I will leave you with this bit of wisdom. Just pick somewhere a really long way away to fly your children to. Fly them out in economy, then fly them back in style. And then tell your children, it's up to them. They will become straight A students, I guarantee you. Or jockeys.

CHAPTER 2

The Korea Cup Part 2

I landed in Seoul late afternoon local time, but my body told me it was around three in the morning. I was met at the airport and driven to the Ambassador Ibis Hotel in downtown. I was going to stay there five nights, this was where the grooms and riders and assistants were staying. When Jack arrived–with Mom–we were all going to check into the Intercontinental, one of Seoul's premier hotels, all courtesy of the Korea Racing Authority. But that was five days in the future, and It only took one evening for my trip to South Korea to become surreal.

I checked in, dumped my belongings, went back down to the lobby, exited the hotel to grab a bottle of water, and walked into an old face from Newmarket. He introduced me to another old face from Newmarket. Water turned to beer. And nothing has been normal since.

We sat outside the hotel in a small seating area. We drank cans of beer, caught up on scandals and gossip from back home, and then we went and dined at KFC. In five years living in Kentucky, I have never felt compelled to enter a KFC. But that first night in Seoul I sat with Steve and Alan from Newmarket eating Kentucky Fried Chicken.

Steve has never been to the States, doesn't know much about it. But he has been to Asia before, worked in Hong Kong for three years exercising horses. An Irish guy he worked with there went to the states, he said. He wondered if I might know him? I tried to explain to him that the USA is huge, that you don't just bump into someone. It turned out that I spent last winter sharing a house with his friend, down in Florida.

The next day it was arranged for me and Ben Correas–son of Argentinian trainer Ignacio to go pick up our horses. Correas and McPeek share one of Keeneland's permanent training barns, so I knew Ben. We were picked up from the hotel and taken to the airport. Things went slowly, but smoothly. I thought Harvey looked pretty pleased to see me, but it's hard to be sure with a horse –and to be honest, he tends to look pretty pleased to see anyone who is prepared to clean his stall and make his dinner.

It was a one-hour van ride back to the track. Once there I bathed him, walked him for a while, settled him in his stall, took his temperature, which is important–shipping fever is a serious issue, and can be, in rare instances, deadly. He was fine. I arranged for him to get some IV fluids to help hydrate him quickly and gave him his dinner.

Back at the hotel, the French contingent showed up. They have a runner in the Korea Sprint, the other international race that takes place Sunday. Their exercise rider was Italian. I have no idea how, but 20 minutes later I was face-timing with Tony "Chicken" Polli from Sardinia–who years ago was apprenticed to me in Newmarket, and now worked in the same stable–in France, as this Italian guy,

Guiseppe. I was getting a bit disorientated. It was the drink, the body clock out, the strange sights and smells, the fading light. I went to bed.

The next afternoon Juliette, who is over with the Tom Amoss team, asked me if I had seen the video Jack posted on Instagram. I don't use Instagram. She showed me a video of Jack on one knee, in a restaurant, obviously proposing to a girl, who is obviously saying yes. I knew Jack was seeing a girl down in Henderson while he was riding at Ellis Park, but I thought they had just been on a few dates. I had never met her, neither had Vicky–as far as I knew anyway. I didn't say much, just pondered it a bit and finished looking after the horse.

In the cab on the way back to the hotel with Ben I ask him to look up Jack's Instagram page. He does, and nearly jumps through the cab roof. When I see Ben's reaction I suddenly realize that I must be underreacting, so I start going crazy too. "But Jack's normally so sensible!?" Ben kept crying. We couldn't work it out.

We get back to the hotel. I sprint across the road and pick up a bottle of Absolut. Steve, Alan, and Guiseppe are there. A stewards enquiry is held. It goes on a long time. It was too late to call Jack or Vicky, I would just have to wait till morning. After another drink my patience ran out. I started texting the hell out of him.

A free dessert. That's what they got, him and the girl. A free dessert, for making a spoof engagement video. Very funny.

"What is the matter with you?!" was his reply. I still don't know.

Traffic and food. These are problems in Seoul. It is a city of 10 million people, expect traffic. But it is really heavy sometimes. Our taxi ride twice daily to and from the racetrack is an ordeal. Two hours a day minimum in a taxi. Sometimes one leg can take the best part of an hour. In fact it is maybe wrong to even call it a taxi ride. It feels more like getting into the taxi waiting for us outside the track, then sitting there, and waiting until continental drift has brought our hotel to within walking distance, and then getting back out again.

I have been here five days now. My dinners have been: KFC, Pizza Hut, Papa John's, Papa John's, McDonalds. I want to eat the local cuisine, I have to eat the local cuisine in order to write about it. But it is terrifying looking, and the smell of the food in the air is strong and pungent and just doesn't smell like any food I have known. I have never thought of myself as a fussy eater, I can eat the hottest curry known to man. But when you see the pictures of food on the menus, my courage leaves me. I have no idea what they are, but one looked like say, eyeball in rich blood stew. Another looked like one of those shots you get from an internal surgical camera.

So, I get my Starbucks at lunchtime, and eat junk food in the evening, and drink an Absolut in the night. And marvel at the world. I talk about it sometimes with Harvey when I am giving him his afternoon constitutional. How we have flown a third of the way around the world, and we are both eating and drinking the same as we would at home. That it is just the proportions that change. That here in Seoul there is more Korean food and less McDonalds, while back in Lexington there is more McDonalds and less Korean food. But in both places it is all available. All the cuisines, everywhere. That's a good thing, blending is good, mixing. It has been good to come here, to mix with other people, other cultures.

To experience their city, and to look at their food.

CHAPTER 3

The Korea Cup Part 3

It's Saturday, the eve of the Keeneland Korea Cup. Jack arrived this morning at 4 a.m.; his flight went smoothly, luckily dodging the typhoon that started blowing into Seoul just after lunchtime. Flights are being cancelled now, but the horse and jockey are here.

Harvey Wallbanger (Congrats) completed his training this morning. He has trained well, is acting well. He is eating everything I give him. But we won't know, until the race, how he will get on with this track. I think that may be the biggest factor, for all the international horses, how they get on with the track. The track here is sand, just sand. The kickback is significant, it fans into the air when the horses kick into it. I don't think Harvey would like having too much sand kicked into his face. He's not that kind of horse.

It is getting exciting now, everyone is ready now. I checked into the Intercontinental hotel yesterday. It is nice, plush, big. The rooms are swanky, but I can't make anything work. The lights are a mystery to me. I have been getting around using the torch on my iPhone.

The toilet has an array of controls and buttons next to it. I have no idea what they do. I was scared to sit on it. This thing looks like it might do something unexpected. I stared at it. Why does a toilet need a control panel? I have a history with toilets. I didn't want a history with them, but I have one. I found the flusher, on the side, as normal. That reassured me, I sat down. The seat was warm, I stood up. I didn't like that. Had room service just come in and used my room for their convenience? I don't like to sit down on a warm pan. It was a heated seat. A heated pan seat! I suppose when you are staying in a hotel that charges you over 30 dollars for a sandwich, they really want to look after you.

Jack fixed the lights for me, then we headed down to the racetrack. A racetrack, at the end of the day, is a racetrack. They come in different shapes and sizes. Seoul racetrack is big, functional, not beautiful, but not ugly. It is a bit like a pretty decent airport.

Seoul itself is big, functional, not beautiful, but not ugly. What is a bit beautiful are the people. I'm not talking about their looks, although they are actually quite handsome. I mean they are composed, seem confident, they have treated us, everywhere, with almost chivalric politeness. Their bow is not subservient, it is an acknowledgement of another person. They are quietly efficient, and when you need something, or ask about something. They don't stand there slack jawed scratching their recently heated behind. They are on it straight away.

I stood in the rain one afternoon, waiting for the lights to change to cross the road. A man came and stood next to me, he put his umbrella over me, and he asked me where I was walking to. My hotel was only across the way, he walked with me right up to the entrance.

He didn't have to; my genes are Irish, I don't really notice the rain. But I was touched by that. In a city of 10 million people, a local saw a foreign stranger, and offered to help him, quite unbidden. Think about that, us wall builders, us Brexiteers, us westerners.

I didn't know what to expect when I came to the Republic of Korea. I think I found the future. The Koreans, are hardworking, polite, working together, helping even strangers. Many speak English. They are doing their thing. They drive Mercedes Benzes and Porsches, and party till dawn at the weekend. They are confident. Koreans enjoy some of the best education and healthcare in the world. It is innovative, growing, progressive, and as far as I can tell, harmonious. It has the 11th largest economy in the world by nominal GDP. And is reckoned to have the seventh-largest betting turnover in the world. That turnover provided the purses for Sunday's race. And, as usual, us westerners have come to plunder.

But at least we have been invited this time. We were invited by the Korea Racing Authority. They have flown us in style, put us up in the best hotels, and their team at the racetrack could not have been friendlier or more efficient, and fun. They are young, the people at the track who manage our quarantine barn, and they are friendly, and patient and courteous–even with Peter Walder, who, as a fellow contrarian, I can only look on and admire, as he carves his pretty unique path through life.

When I woke up in Seoul at 3 a.m. last Friday morning, I watched Jack riding the Thursday card at Kentucky Downs live. I was in the future.

CHAPTER 4

The Keeneland Korea Cup Part 4

The writing was on the wall after the Korea Sprint. There were three North American runners. They never figured, hardly drew a mention, couldn't find top gear on the deep sandy track.

We kept hoping though. You have to have hope. Harvey Wallbanger had taken the whole trip in his stride. The flight, the long hours traveling, the morning training, the walk to the racetrack, the 60,000 onlookers. He took it all in his stride Harvey, never left an oat, drank plenty of water, trained nicely. He is a nice easygoing character. He bit me three times since we have been here, but they were playful nips, just his way of telling me it's lunchtime.

Jack came in the paddock wearing silks of purple diamonds. Mom led the horse, it was like the old days back in Newmarket. Coming out of the first turn the horse in front of him got tightened up and his jockey pulled him back, Jack had to pull back too, but Harvey still took a bump, after that it rained sand the whole way, he turned into the straight nearly last, then found a bit when Jack asked him, he moved up to sixth, but that was as much as he could muster on that sandy track, it turned out that was the best that any of the five American raiders could muster that day.

I was disappointed for connections, but overall it has been great. The 3am wake ups have been wearying, each day we were all more tired than the day before. The traffic is everywhere making the constant taxi rides an ordeal. But South Korea won the Korea Cup. One for the locals, winning their own international invitational. That was a big step forward for Korean racing. After the race, back at the barn, the staff who had been helping us these past days seemed subdued. Ben asked them, weren't they pleased a local horse had won? They told him, but we have been with all of you, with your horses. We wanted you to do well.

The experience has been great. It was enjoyable, interesting, fun. The people were helpful and hospitable and warm. As for the food, well representatives of Keeneland and Korea Racing Authority were kind enough to take us out for dinner after the race. They knew where to eat and what to order. Apparently Korean barbecue is a big thing, everywhere, even in the States, that passed me by.. It was really good. We had pork belly pieces cooked over a small charcoal pit right there on the table. We had side dishes with sesame leaf, garlic, chilies. We had a spicy soup, we had Kimchi…that's what that smell was! Cabbage soaked in chili, it was fine, the rest was excellent. For dessert I thought I'd eat some humble pie. I always seem to be eating that stuff lately. I'm surprised I'm not fatter, all the pie I eat.

The next day Harvey was flying home. I arranged for him to have more IV fluids before his flight, to ensure maximal hydration.

Harry (Hyungmin Che) helped me, he was one of our interpreters for the week. We talked about football, the premier league in the UK, Liverpool football team – his favorite. He knew more about it all than me. It turned out he was educated at an English boarding school in Switzerland. We talked about the States, that he hoped to come over for the Kentucky Derby next year. We friended on Facebook so I could show him around if he does. It turns out he spent four years attending college in Washington DC. It's been like that, the whole trip. Sometimes the further you travel, the closer you realize you are to home. John Lennon wrote a song about it all once.

It's been a whirlwind, well actually, a typhoon. Korea, I bow to you.

CHAPTER 5

Came the Dark Horse

He was the first Thoroughbred I ever bought. I purchased him at auction on one bid for four hundred and fifty guineas. And they threw in the devil for free.

A neat little yearling colt with a coat as black as the coals that stoke the fires of hell. "Cheap, small, and common" would be the dismissive consensus of the experts. Perhaps they forgot that his line went back to Northern Dancer, and that Northern Dancer, champion racehorse, legendary sire, was also passed over as too small as a yearling by the experts.

Black horses sometimes seem to have a bit more temperament than the average racehorse. And this little yearling turned into a blackguard two-year-old. Strong willed, unwilling to submit, acknowledging no one as his master. He would rear, and spin, and buck, and run backward as often as forward; he would dive off the gallops, plunging. And he grew big and muscular and strong, and he had eyes like an eagle's, predatory, unafraid. Never afraid. Never shying or running from a sudden noise or a startling scene. He was the Alpha of alpha males.

Eventually, somehow, he accepted enough of what I asked him to do that I thought he was ready to race. It was a big day for me, my first ever runner in a race. A horse I had bought and broken and ridden and trained and groomed and fed and cared for. I had clung on when he'd tried to throw me, and I had escaped most of his open-mouthed lunges at my arms and dodged most of his raised, jabbing, threatening hind legs, which would arc and slowly circle, like a Yankees' batsman waiting to let loose his biggest swing.

He took two strides out onto the track with the jockey on his back, and he reared to his fullest height. The jockey was dislodged, and the blackguard took off. The race was delayed while we sped around the course in the back of a Range Rover to catch him. I found him on the far side; he had his head down eating grass. *Fuck you,* he said. *You don't own me. I call the shots here.* He never did misbehave on the racetrack again. He was just letting me know that it was his choice to race, not mine.

But boy, could he run. Just a month after that debacle, he disposed of a useful field of two-year-old maidens at Royal Windsor Racecourse. And then, just fading late after setting a blistering early pace, he finished fifth in the richest two-year-old handicap of the year. He was clocked traveling at forty-three miles an hour that day, with the rider sat back hauling on the reins against him.

For the next two years, this dark beast and I fought for dominance. He became even tougher to deal with, dangerous sometimes. I was younger and braver then, and experienced with Thoroughbreds, so mostly I didn't get too scared. Mostly. But he kept racing; he channelled that aggression, that inner rage, that desire for dominance into performance on the racetrack. You could see it in the way he stretched at the gallop, his head horizontal, pushing himself to the limit, every ounce of him determined to best his foes.

He rewarded us with strings of valiant efforts in good races at the top racetracks in the country. Newmarket, Ascot, Haydock, York, we went to them all, pitching him against expensive horses from the big, established stables, beating more of them than beat us. Giving us great excitement, great days, great moments. Cheering, shouting, punching the air, hugging, congratulating, laughing. Adrenaline- fueled celebrations.

By four he had become dangerous to be around. A brooding monster, stalking around his caged stall. Malevolent. Looking for a fight. He would rear in his stable and put his feet against the wall, to look down with blazing eyes on his cowering neighbour in the next stall. He would pick up his feed manger and hurl it over the wall out into the walkway. His teeth were weapons now; a rag or a stick was needed to engage them whenever he was handled. He was powerful now. A magnificent beast. An alpha male in his prime, with an alpha male's aggression.

I had him castrated that spring. It is a bigger job when they are older, a lot of blood is spilt. But he recovered well. He still remained a handful, willful, tough and ornery, and still aggressive—except with Jack. When the boy walked up to him, the horse would lower his big head and allow him to push his toy stethoscope up into one of his velvet nostrils, and he would allow him to stroke his silken nose, and his ears would be pricked the whole time, seemingly mesmerized by this tiny child.

For the rest of us, though, the ears stayed pinned back. But at least he stopped rearing, and the anger, the rage at his captivity, subsided slightly, and he continued to channel his aggression into his races.

Indeed, he even raced better, year after year, winning and placing all over the country. Until, at the age of seven, he won his first stakes race. The JRA Nakayama Rous Stakes at Newmarket racetrack. Our home. He was 50/1 in the morning betting, and he won by a nose. I remember waiting the eternal wait for the result of the photo finish. "First, number ten, Rushcutter Bay..." I choked up, couldn't talk as people grabbed me. It is still etched in my soul all these years later. Something I had done, something I had achieved. No money, no connections, no father. Yet somehow, someway, I was standing there as a trainer in the winner's enclosure for a major race, at one of the most historic racetracks in the world. It was nothing in the great scheme of things of course. But it was everything to me.

And the best was yet to come. The following spring, he followed up in the Group 3 Palace House Stakes, back on the Rowley Mile, on 2000 Guineas Day. The spring sun shining, tens of thousands of spectators, and legendary jockey Mick Kinane in the saddle.

He did it well that day, a flash of black tearing down on the slighter, grey filly in the lead; he thundered past her, opening up as he hit the final hill. The dominant winner. At that moment, the highest rated sprinter in Europe. Champagne. Dreams of Royal Ascot. Looking forward to Longchamp on Arc day for his first Group 1 contest. All that he gave us in return for a bucket of feed a few times a day.

He never won another race though. The urge had dimmed a little. He was getting older, passing his prime. The fire that raged inside consumed him less. He was still tough, still trouble, still full of life. But other horses could win the races now. He had fought enough, tried enough, pushed himself enough. He had ruptured enough blood vessels in his lungs, trying to fight for an extra inch or two of flight. He had returned after races with enough of his own blood spilling from his nose. He had tasted victory and defeat enough times now to know those two imposters.

It is over ten years since he ran his last race. I wonder sometimes if he ever remembers. If he ever relives those moments, if they stay with him, as they have stayed with me. Does he think of those days, when he was in his prime, with pride?

Or does he remember being enslaved? Being taken from his mother on that Welsh mountainside he was born and raised on, and sold as "lot 1167, a brown colt." His mother and father, and their mother and father listed on the page...a worthless pedigree to produce a worthless horse...the mare shouldn't have been bred from said the experts. Sold to the young man with the equally damnable pedigree on one bid, for four hundred and seventy pounds. Two longshots brought together. Two strong-willed young males. Each as obstinate as the other.

He was my whale; I was his Ahab. I was the slave master; he was the slave. He fought his enslavement, but I bent him to my will. I had to, you see? There was no other choice for him. He was born a Thoroughbred, an artificial breed, selected for speed, selected for man's sport. He was magnificent, because that is what we bred him to be. So, he could be a racehorse, or he could be nothing. And in the end, he chose to race, to roll like thunder.

But sometimes he haunts me now.

It is twenty-three years since I first saw that small yearling. And I spent nearly every day with him over the next two decades. But I haven't seen him for three years now. And he is four thousand miles away from me. And neither of us are young anymore.

Sometimes now I dream of him being free, a magnificent wild stallion roaming with his herd of mares, mares he had won by fighting for them, by subduing other, lesser foes. And because I am older now,

I see him with his offspring. All of his sons and daughters, all of them beautiful, and proud like him. All of them running together, free like the wind. His superior genes passed on to those descendants, ensuring he would live on, that he would shape the future in some way, that his magnificence would last.

And then one day, when he was past his prime, he would be bested in battle. And he would find somewhere to lay down with his wounds, alone, to die on that mountainside. A wild unconquerable beast, who had lived as God had intended him to live. And was to die as God intended him to die. Unbowed, untamed. Unnamed.

CHAPTER 6

The Triple Crown Part One The Kentucky Derby

I didn't know it at the time, of course. But when I stood beside him at Churchill Downs that morning, I was looking at the horse who would go on to become the first American Triple Crown winner in thirty-seven years.

He stood quietly, waiting at the entrance to the track, waiting his turn to do his morning work. He didn't look special. He looked average, a plain bay, no flashes of white, just a nut-brown coat and a black mane and tail. He was average height for a racehorse, average build, an ok head. He wasn't prancing or snorting; he wasn't surrounded by an entourage, just him and his rider, with his groom at his shoulder, all of them relaxed, slouching slightly, waiting their turn. This was the horse who had just won the Kentucky Derby, standing there, like Rocinante resting from the Spanish sun.

There was only one sign he was special. It was when you looked toward the track. It was when you began to realize that all the other horses, all the other hundreds and hundreds of equine athletes that needed to exercise that morning, were vacating the track. And then the track was harrowed. And then, when it was empty, and silent, and pristine, that was when American Pharoah went out, with the track to himself, to exercise. And then there was nothing ordinary or average about him at all.

It is his stride that marks him out. He has the stride of a bigger horse, the stride of a longer, more powerful horse. He moves like gravity presses down less on him than others. His stride is fluent and perfect and powerful and long. And it doesn't falter, it doesn't weaken, it doesn't yield. Even when his mile gallop was over, the stride kept propelling him along while his rider struggled to ease him down.

There is a period of suspension when a horse gallops. A period when all four legs are off the ground simultaneously, when the horse is just gliding forward through the air, legs tucked beneath him. American Pharoah seemed to spend longer in this phase than other horses. You don't have to be an expert when you watch American Pharoah gallop to know he is good.

I was at the derby. It was ferocious. The huge grandstand under the twin spires seats seventy thousand people, an unbelievable number for a racetrack. And that left another hundred thousand standing.

It is a long day. The first race goes off before noon, but the derby itself isn't run until nearly seven in the evening. It is nearly two hours from the race before the Derby until the event itself. But time doesn't drag, there is always something to catch your eye, some moment to get caught up in. The horses, the races, the noise, the people, the clothes, the hats. Shouting, cheering, laughter, talking, posing, eating, drinking too much, spending too much, getting lost in the moment. Escaping for a while. For a day.

Eventually it was time. The horses entered the paddock. This was the first time I had ever seen him in the flesh. The horse who was destined for greatness, marked out. The chosen one. The special one. He didn't prance or dance, he knew what his job was, he knew what was to come; he was to do what he'd been bred for, and I could see in his eye he was ready.

From an initial debut defeat at Del Mar the previous summer, he had racked up four consecutive wins, three of them grade one events, as high as you can go. But this was the Kentucky Derby. The big one. The greatest two minutes in sport.

Field sizes on the dirt in America seldom get close to their maximum of twelve runners, and races rarely exceed a mile in length. The derby this year had eighteen runners due to go to post and would be run over a distance of a mile and a quarter.

For those familiar with the Epsom Derby, you might say, *So what?* After all, that event has large fields and is run over a mile and a half. But dirt racing is not like turf racing. Not one little bit. There is no conservation of energy on dirt, no bounce, no springing off the lush sward. Dirt is dirt, it lays there soft on top until they hit the hard clay base beneath. No spring, no bounce, stamina sapping, leg weakening, jarring, hard, unforgiving, uncaring, brutal, tough. And it sprays up from the horses' hooves, kicking into the faces of the runners and riders behind, stinging them, blinding them, discouraging them, disheartening them, beating them. And all the while one hundred and seventy thousand people look on, roaring, their faces red, their fists clenched, primitive, uncivilized, aggressive. The biggest mob on Earth, lost in each blurring moment.

And then he won. He fought hard, he ran with the leaders, his rider's silks were clean as a victors' should be, the others dirty and brown and beaten. But he was tired. He had won, but he had fought hard for his victory. He had shown heart and courage and toughness. Traits that Americans like. Like an American Pharaoh.

So, he came back to the baying mob, and now they were cheering, and smiling, and clapping. The mob was sated, satisfied. Their champion had emerged victorious from the battle, from the violent encounter. He was tired, but unscathed and victorious.

And even as The Roses were placed around his neck, people began to ask, people who knew horses, people who could see. They asked. *Could this be the one?*

CHAPTER 7

The Triple Crown Part Two The Preakness

The day dawned overcast. The clouds were heavy, and low, and ominous. The 140th Preakness Stakes was due to be run the afternoon of May 16, 2015, two weeks to the day after American Pharoah had emerged victorious in the Kentucky Derby. The Preakness is the older race by two years, and although its younger brother outshines it in every way now, Pimlico Race Course was still expecting a crowd of a hundred thousand to come and see the horse attempt to win the second leg of the Triple Crown.

Expectation weighed heavy on the event, on American Pharoah's connections, on the American race fans. The rain fell. The clouds sunk lower, and heavier, and darker. The dirt turned to mud. But the people came. The drink flowed. And in the infield, the kids grew raucous. And in the grandstand, those with the best seats, those with the connections and the money, they dressed in their finery, and drank their Black-Eyed Susans, and everyone waited.

Everyone knew what was coming. Everyone knew that no matter how many contests were carded that day, there was only one race, one test that mattered. *It should be a formality,* they said. *He can't be beat,* they said. Well, they can get beat. They can all get beat. There is sometimes a David to defeat Goliath, it happens. And this is a horse race, it is gladiatorial, tough, fast. Dangerous. Beautiful poetry can turn into ugly chaos in an instant.

You see the jockeys when they come into the paddock, their diminutive size a surprise to first timers—even though they knew. Their colourful silks in a myriad of hues and patterns, their jaunty walk, special to them, owed to the development of muscles of the thighs and calves, necessary to squat like a downhill skier behind the horse's mane. They can look like a little troop of players, of clowns even. And when they meet the trainers and owners, they smile and joke, and they seem as if they have not a care in the world. But if you look closer; if you look closer you will see the focus in their eyes. And if you look, you will see their demeanour change as the call for jockeys up is given. You will see a steeliness set in as they are legged up, and they lock their legs to the young Thoroughbred. And then suddenly, they look regal, and the spectators look small and insignificant and dull compared to these men on these animals. Suddenly they look special. Suddenly everyone can see who they are, and what they can do.

Of course, for the big races, for a race like this, the jockeys room will change. The atmosphere will pervade the room, hour by hour, slowly, hardly perceptible at first, but then, as the time approaches, the riders thoughts turn to the big one. And they change out of the silks from the previous race, and their torsos are taut and lean and muscular, and for some of them, then, their scars are exposed. Some are small, some minor incident. But some are deep and terrible. Some awful battle, some moment when carnage reigned, and people and horses were hurt. They were hurt. But they recovered, and they returned to the battle. They would not be cowed or bowed. Because they are brave, because this is what they do, because this is what they feel compelled to do. Because the glory of the win, the urge for victory, is greater than the fear of the pain, for now at least.

So, they carry on time and time again, and sometimes on days like this, they get to be a part of history. Their names shall be written in the history books of the sport. And a hundred years from now, people may look and wonder who these people were, and what was life like back then.

The sky was grey, and black, and low, and wet, and the track was muddy. And as the riders prepared for the race, great, deep, heavy footsteps of thunder rocked everything. Lightning flashed, and rain threw itself down upon the Earth. The infield was emptied of people, and when the storm lessened, the horses and jockeys paraded out onto the flooded, muddy, dirty track. Everything was grey and wet. The riders' colourful silks subdued by the wet air, by the grey sky, and in the race, by the flying mud.

He broke out of the gates well and took the lead by the first turn, his seven competitors fanned out behind him. He travelled easily through the water and mud along the backstretch and entered the home turn in command. But the time had been fast early, and the conditions were testing, and he was just a three-year-old Thoroughbred, powerful but fragile. It isn't over just because they enter the stretch in front, now it takes talent, it takes heart, it takes everything. And as the commentator was drowned out by the roaring crowd, he came, a gold and turquoise beast emerging from the primordial soup, from the water and the muddy earth from which everything was born. And each furious stride sent curtains of dirt high into the air, spraying the sky. Declaring himself its master.

And as he crossed the line, everything became one.

CHAPTER 8

The Triple Crown Part Three The Belmont Stakes

I was at Indiana Grand Racing and Casino on Saturday, June 6, 2015. The day of the 147th running of the Belmont Stakes. The day American Pharoah was to face his greatest test.

The mile and a half route, over the large Belmont Park oval, is an extreme distance on dirt, and there was little guarantee on pedigree that the Kentucky Derby and Preakness winner could last out the extra two furlongs. Further than he had ever run before. Further than any of them had ever run before. For the eight runners due to go to post shortly before seven p.m. New York time, this was going to be the most exhausting day of their lives.

I have spent a lot of time at Indiana Grand. Jack rides there often during the summer. It is a long drive there, and when you arrive, it is uninspiring, strictly business, more about the casino than the racing. Hardly anyone watches the racing, except on Saturdays, when they race in the evening. Then people come and eat barbecue and drink beer and bet the ponies. This Saturday, though, you couldn't move. All of Indiana was there. They were there to watch the Belmont Stakes.

About an hour before the big race I went down into the casino; it was humming, but I was able to grab a lone stool at the sports bar. From there I could watch the boy race and also watch Belmont Park.

The sky was blue in New York, and due to crowd concerns, for the first time, the venue had limited itself to ninety thousand tickets sold. They were all taken before the day of the event. I had seen the crowd before for the Belmont. I had seen them before with a Triple Crown contender. Crazy crowds, loud, boisterous, drunk, hollering and shouting. Wild. And I had seen the disappointment before, when the wrong horse won, when the Triple Crown went unclaimed for another year. It had been unclaimed for thirty-seven years now.

I got talking to the guy next to me at the bar, the way you do. I asked him what he liked for the big one, what he thought about American Pharoah.

"That horse won't stay!" he exclaimed aggressively. "I've taken the field against him, exactas, trifectas, superfectas. That horse won't win today!"

I looked down in front of him; there was a tall pile of tickets next to his beer. I didn't say anything. The man seemed agitated, maybe he had staked too much, maybe he had drunk too much. Maybe both.

Except for the distance and the weather, the race was a rerun of the Preakness. American Pharoah slightly missed the break but had secured the lead by the first turn. Along the backstretch, I marvelled again at his stride, so powerful and fluent and long, and I knew then that a stride like that would break his competitors, before it faltered itself.

He turned into the long Belmont homestretch on a tight rein still, and Frosted made an attempt to draw up to him, to challenge him, to make a race of it. There was no use, though, he was too good. He was born too good. And as his rider shook the reins at him and sent him to the wire, he opened up and lengthened his stride, and he extended his lead, and the crowd was delirious, and the commentator was screaming and hoarse with excitement, and the bar erupted. And as he passed the wire, the first Triple Crown winner since 1978, the man next to me was crying "No! No! NO!" in despair.

There have been over seven hundred thousand Thoroughbred colt foals born in North America since the crop in which Affirmed, the last Triple Crown winner, was born in 1975. He was ridden by a quiet, modest, charming kid from Kentucky. "The Kentucky Kid." He was just eighteen years old when he won the Triple Crown on Affirmed. The same age my son, also a jockey, was when American Pharoah won the Triple Crown. But my son was riding lesser horses at Indiana that night, he is waiting for his shot, for his big horse still. But he is young. It isn't often you get a shot to star as young as Steve Cauthen was all those years ago. It was the rider who seemed born for greatness in the 1978 Triple Crown series. In the 2015 Triple Crown, it was the horse who was born for greatness.

American Pharoah has just been better than the seven hundred thousand other colts that came along since Affirmed. There had been plans for all of them when they were born. Hopes. Dreams. Some were realized, to a lesser or greater extent. Many were disappointments, failures who could not live up to the dreams placed on them, unwittingly, unknowingly. They tried but they could not succeed.

And how many people were born in that time, how many dreams did they have, how many succeeded, and how many failed? What of my friend at the bar? What dreams had his parents had for him when he was born, what aspirations were there?

Or were there none? Was he cursed from birth? Did no one love him properly, or care for him deeply, or dream for him greatly? Was he destined to be miserable, to hope for failure in others? Or had he tried? Had he tried like American Pharoah's opponents, but was found wanting? Did he find that he just couldn't fulfill his dreams in any measure? That he didn't have what it took, that he just couldn't make it?

Greatness strikes rarely. It is not failure to not win. Gallant Frosted in second was not a failure. The seventeen talented horses and riders strung out behind the great one in the Kentucky Derby were not failures. They were not failures because they were still trying, still fighting, still in the game, playing the game. Making the game.

But people shouldn't bet against the great ones, equine or human. The great ones may lose battles here and there, but, in the end, eventually, they tend to win the wars. That is why most people cheer for them, and love them, and applaud them. Like I did.

And it made the hair on the back of my neck stand up as he crossed the line, because finally, American Pharoah, after all those years, after all that waiting, he really was *The One*.

CHAPTER 9

Ripper and the Biscuit

New Orleans is different to everywhere else. It is like three continents got thrown into a tumble dryer and were spun all around. And one got pulled out, and at its bottom edge was a splash of colour, and that was New Orleans.

It is ghost stories and voodoo, and horse drawn carriages and trams, and old-world cobbled streets with rows of tiny shuttered houses, it is cozy corner restaurants and intimate shadowy jazz bars. And music draws you everywhere and around the next corner you may find a ragged old man dancing or a young woman singing and from one moment to the next you don't know if you will fall in love or have your wallet taken. I almost fancy saying, that if you haven't been to New Orleans, you haven't really been anywhere.

I have flown down to this place, to visit two sons of Newmarket, born and raised. And now they are here in this urban fantasyland, plying their trade as jockeys, far from the eternal Heath. And I am here to find out, why?

I have known Adam Beschizza, now twenty-seven, since he first rode out the odd lot for me when a little shy of his sixteenth birthday. My son Jack Gilligan, who picked me up from the airport is twenty-three now, he rode his first racehorse out for me on Newmarket heath when he was thirteen.

They have followed similar paths the two jockeys. Adam rode out every day before school, for his aunt, Julia Feilden, Jack each day, for me. Apparently, Adam got paid for his toils. At fourteen they both elected to take the Flexible Learning Programme offered at the British Racing School. A two-year course, which necessitated them missing one day of school each week, both of them liked the idea of that, and both of them finished top of their respective class.

Upon finishing school Adam became apprenticed to Ed Dunlop. Jack left school a few years later. The USA had been on Jack's mind since a student exchange between the British Racing School and its North American equivalent found Jack spending a week with legendary ex-North American jockey Chris McCarron. Chris showed Jack around Lexington Kentucky, they went to Keeneland races, visited Zenyatta, ate out at night, met the great and the good, and he came back and told his parents he was going to be a jockey in America. I insisted that, having been raised in the town, he must spend a year with a major trainer in Newmarket first, and so I arranged for him to be apprenticed to Sir Mark Prescott.

Roll on a year, and Sir Mark Prescott's yard broom proved no match as a lure when set against the rolling hills of Kentucky, and the opportunity to maybe turbo charge his career American style.

Jack flew out of Heathrow late August 2014, with his parents in tow, four wins from twenty-six rides under his belt – his last ride in the UK was a winner, and a green card granted through my American citizenship. I was as interested to see the place as he was.

By this time Adam had just finished his solid apprenticeship in the UK and was experiencing the usual dip in mounts and winners often experienced by young riders just entering the professional ranks. By the following year he was fighting back in style, capturing the autumn double of the Cambridgeshire and the Cesarewitch handicaps on his home turf. He had already spent one winter in the USA by now though, riding track work at the Fair Grounds, and the seed of a plan had been planted.

By the time Adam joined Jack in the USA in 2017, Jack had ridden nearly two hundred winners stateside. Adam wasted no time catching up though, thanks in no small part to a new up and coming trainer by the name of Joe Sharp who Adam had befriended when they both rode trackwork for the same trainer during his winter stint in the States.

Us three Newmarketeers are sat outside CC's coffee house in Bayou St John, around the corner from the track, relaxing under a mighty oak, – giant trees, found all around, ancient trees, with twisting arms and Spanish moss draped over them like tinsel. There is a light breeze and the morning sun is just starting to make itself felt. I am sat with those two boys now, who used to ride out for me in Newmarket, on the Heath, one of them unpaid.

Jack has ridden over 300 winners stateside now, he has ridden four Stakes winners also, including two Grade (Group) 3's this year. His career mounts earnings are closing in on eight million dollars now. Adam, in little over two years here is just shy of 250 winners stateside, his mounts have already netted over ten million dollars, he has picked up four Grade 3's and a couple of minor Stakes, and he sits next to us now as Fair Grounds leading rider of the 2018/19 season. He is the champion here Adam. And he is back to defend his crown.

Jack says he doesn't dwell on England much now, he has been here five years, that is a long time at 23. He was seventeen when he left England, left Newmarket. I have a lot of memories still, of there, most of my memories are there, training horses for nearly two decades, struggling for most of it. Jack is making memories here.

Adam says he misses his mates, you don't rip into your friends here, don't bond as closely. Anyway, he came here for business not pleasure. He wanted to ride winners and make money. It was the same for Jack. They are hard workers both of them, and when I speak to them, I see something in their eyes, but I'm not sure what yet.

They were both always going to be jockeys they said, they just always knew, it was simple. Adam says he remembers before he left school, looking in amazement at the kids who said they didn't know what they wanted to do. Whenever the subject of exams came up in our home – and some of Jack's family are academic highflyers, he would tell his parents, what do I need them for? I'm going to be a jockey.

But still, it isn't a straight line, a smooth upward ascent for most, even the ones that make it. Kieren Fallon didn't even ride out his claim. But Kieren kept grafting, I think he knew inside he had it. So, they have both worked, both grafted, they aren't the wild ones, on an adrenaline rush after racing. I have seen Jack go home after riding a treble, have a hot chocolate and then go to bed. Adam is the same. It's business, a business they were born into. It may seem glamorous to some from the outside looking in. But to them it's their job, and they work, as everyone does, for their pay cheque.

I don't know what Adam picked up last week. But Jack had a cheque, waiting by his peg in the jockeys room for $5,600 for his previous weeks efforts at the Fair Grounds, That was opening weekend, he rode two winners, an above average cheque, but just above average, he gets plenty of cheques like that. He likes them, they both do, all jockeys do. There are expenses here though. Jockeys agents are more hands on here, they prowl the barns trying to sell their jockeys in the mornings, they hustle, and they charge their riders 25% of their career earnings for that. I don't like jockey agents. The valet's get 5% too. But the valets are the jockeys friends, confidants, advisors and carers. I like the valets.

They race four days a week at Fair Grounds, Thursday through Sunday. Opening day is wild, all the locals come, and they dress up in crazy outfits like it's Mardi Gras. Louisiana Derby Day in March is busy too. A million-dollar race, they have both ridden in it. Most days though the crowd is just a healthy spattering, there are locals here, barflies of the racetrack. Adam's nickname "biscuit" travelled with him. The locals decided to find one for Jack. A kind good-hearted gentleman called Terrance, known to his friends as Forty-Niner, started shouting him "Jack the Ripper!" Someone else started shouting him "CrackerJack." The Ripper is sticking at the moment down here.

I asked Adam about winning the riding title here last year, what it meant to him. Did it mean a lot? It did he said, but it was hard, he found it hard, worked hard. For as many horses you may ride in the afternoon a jockey in the USA may ride as many in the mornings, they are the test pilots, called in for the fast work. The horses will be ready and tacked for them, one after another, breezing (galloping) them in hard succession. The most Jack breezed in a morning was ten, at Keeneland, a few years ago. They don't get paid for them, but they do get the ride in the race.

So, Adam, vying for the title, taking as many mounts as the agent could get him, breezing as many as could be hustled, he worked, and he sweated, and he rode. He rode 86 winners at the Fair Grounds last winter, in just over four months. His mounts earnt around $2.5 million. He was the champ now. The leading rider down here in The Big Easy.

Nouvelle Orleans was claimed by the French in 1718, then released to the Spanish, then returned to the French, then sold by Bonaparte himself. He sold New Orleans, and the surrounding territories to the relatively recently formed United States in 1803. It was a place where great fortunes were built on sugar and cotton and slavery, and where the descendants of French and Spanish and French Canadian and other European blood mixed.

Fair Grounds may not be familiar to race fans in the UK, but it is no small meet, no chicken feed meet. Florent "Frenchie" Geroux – Breeders Cup and Pegasus World Cup winning jockey winters here. So does Robby Albarado, Curlin's Jockey, a lot of the Kentucky jockey colony moves down here for the winter. Many multiple Grade one winning riders winter here.

The Fair Grounds started racing in 1872, it is one of the more historic tracks in North America. But the Europeans, and the Cajuns – descendants of French Canadians, had been racing horses for a century before that. Cajuns are noted horsemen in the States. Robby Albarado, Calvin Borel, Kent Desormeaux, and plenty of others learned their craft riding bush races as twelve-year-old kids.

Many legendary names in North American racing have won riding titles here, and now the name Adam Beschizza sits with them. A name that could almost pass for Cajun too.

I went racing at Fair Grounds the following day, Adam and Jack had four rides each. Adam managed a second, Jack a third, a quiet day, just business as usual. I watched them go about their job, immersed in it now, both of them known by everyone here. Adam may have the riding title, but Jack has the better nickname. I met some familiar faces, I spent the past two years as assistant to a leading Kentucky trainer, I was his assistant at Keeneland, at Saratoga, we won a couple of Grade ones, had runners and places in the Breeders Cup.

Maiden races run here at Fair Grounds offer over thirty thousand pounds in prize money. Back in Kentucky last month, maiden races were offering over seventy thousand pounds in prize money. That is pretty big money whichever way you look at it.

I went out with Jack after racing, we took the tram down to the French Quarter, it is quaint and old, and beautiful, like a picturesque old town in Europe, and it is real. No *Mcdonalds* here. The best food I have ever eaten is here, in the quaintest restaurants, with the coolest vibe. We went to a little place called the Orleans Grapevine, small, French-like. We sat at the bar and had a glass of champagne, a piano played behind us without a piano player. The bartender gave us a bowl of crispy streaky bacon (a genius idea in my opinion) and we talked. I talked to my son, I don't often get him to myself now, he is busy, and so have I been, our jobs left us often a thousand miles apart.

I asked him what was the best thing about being in the States? His V8 5 litre Ford F150 pick-up truck was his answer – he likes his cars. It is a hulking brute of a vehicle, terrifying to our European scaled eyes when we first arrived and saw them, but they quickly became objects of desire in Jack's. I thought I saw something else in his eyes though, again, and this time I think I worked it out. His eyes are older. They are serious, they are not the eyes of a kid, carefree, silly. Jack and Adam have the eyes of soldiers in the field. There is work to be done, tough work, dangerous work sometimes, and they have chosen to do it. Their fathers weren't wealthy men, they worked out, long ago, as kids maybe, that if they wanted something out of life. If they wanted better things, if they wanted anything really, they would have to go and get it alone. It was the same for me. The sins of the father really are passed on. I think anyway that is what I saw in their eyes. Or perhaps it was just a reflection.

They should be proud of themselves. Adam came here, as did Jack, as do immigrants everywhere, to do better. Well, he did do better, a lot better. I know whatever these two boys were when they left England, that is not what they are now, after thousands of breezes, and thousands of race-rides, after hundreds of winners. I see these two men now, and I wonder, if maybe one day, sometime in the future. If the two boys vanquished from their home, may return, to claim their birthrights as sons of the Newmarket Heath.

CHAPTER 10

Erica Murray

There was a young girl from the small town of Haughton, Louisiana. Her mother, a nurse, would drive her daughter to a babysitter before school, on her way to work. When they passed Louisiana Downs racetrack, the 4-year-old would beg her to stop so they could stand by the rail and watch the horses gallop by.

From that time, the girl determined that one day she would be a jockey riding Thoroughbreds. She had ponies, and she fell off them, but she kept getting back on. She graduated to galloping Thoroughbreds from the tender age of 12, a Cajun tradition it seems.

From 15 she decided online schooling and full-time riding was the right fit for her. "I just went out every morning and begged people to let me gallop, and I just got run off with all the time. But I still remember my first breeze so well. It was just amazing."

She got through school by twisting all her subjects in an equine direction, whether a school essay or a science report, and then spent a season ponying at a Quarter Horse meet.

She stuck at it. "So, as soon as I turned 16, I just went up to the outrider and said 'I'm here to get my jockey license'." And he said, "Who the hell are you?"

In the fall of 2014, aged 17, she went to Fair Grounds to gallop, and a matter of months later obtained her apprentice jockey license. "I was so scared. It was my first time away from home, and I just wanted to make a good impression. I got run off with on my first day."

She didn't race at Fair Grounds that winter, but she learned and gained experience, and on May 9, 2015, she finally donned the silks, at Louisiana Downs, and she won.

"It was so wild. I was literally shaking I was so nervous and excited. I remember in the race, when I got to the eighth pole, the other horses weren't there. I thought something had gone wrong. I cried for about two days after. There were old school friends and my elementary school teachers there."

The next few winners came in just a few weeks, and then a horse ducked and jumped a rail with her. She broke three ribs and punctured her lung, and that meant two months off. Her comeback went well, though. More winners. But then, just a couple of days before the meet ended, two horses went down in front of her and brought her down with them. She suffered severe concussion.

She came back a month or so later, then had another fall, and another concussion, but this one went undiagnosed, and, after that, she kept falling off the horses she exercised. "I was getting lost on the way to work."

Eventually, it took another race spill, knocked out again, before she had the time-out she badly needed. "I went and spent some time in California and recuperated."

On her return, she found rides at Louisiana Downs tough to come by, so she headed up to Indiana Grand and, within a month, found herself in the winner's enclosure once more. But she was having trouble with her left leg going numb. "I was working a horse the morning after the win and, when we were pulling up, I literally dropped on the horse. I had no strength in my back." It took a spinal specialist to diagnose a herniated and crushed disc.

By the time she was ready to race-ride again, Turfway Park had rolled around, but not much happened there, and, when Indiana Grand started in the spring, it was the same story. She decided to head back down to New Orleans and Fair Grounds.

Her first win back came for trainer Denise Schmidt and her partner, Larry 'Deadeye' Jolivette, and business slowly started picking up.

Deadeye had known Murray since she was a kid starting out at Louisiana Downs. He let her gallop for him sometimes, saw how keen she was.

"She had sparkle," he said, "and she was so keen, she would bleed for it."

She won three times on that horse at Fair Grounds, and over the next year she started to ride most of the barn's horses.

And then she broke her arm, and the arm got infected, which kept her out of the saddle for six months.

Finally, last year, things clicked. "2019 was my best year to date. I went to Evangeline and won six from about 20 mounts. Then I won about 11 at Louisiana, and then I came to Fair Grounds.

"I got here and people were telling me not to give up my galloping job."

She has ridden 14 winners so far at the meet. Fair Grounds has a competitive jockey colony, and 22-year-old Murray is lying 18th, one behind Edgar Morales, in number of wins.

There was a jumps trainer in England, Captain Tim Forster. He had a runner in the Grand National. He didn't think the horse was much of a jumper, which was quite important as it is a 4¼-mile race with 30 five-foot obstacles to overcome. He didn't think much of the jockey either. When they were in the paddock, the rider asked the trainer for his instructions. "Keep remounting," he told him. They won the race.

Erica Murray has kept remounting.

CHAPTER 11

Black Gold

There is a horse buried in the infield at Fair Grounds in New Orleans. A famous horse, with an interesting story. His racing career commenced and ended at Fair Grounds, but his tale began with his mother.

The Thoroughbred filly foal was born, somehow, in Oklahoma, in the then Indian territory in 1907. Although a registered Thoroughbred, most of her 34 career victories were gained in informal unregistered bush races, match races, but she did win under rules.

The last time she ever ran a race, her owner, who doted on her, had been convinced to enter her for a claiming contest in Juarez, Mexico, with a $5,000 tag. His trainer had spoken with connections of the other contestants and was assured no-one would claim her as the owner's love and attachment for the filly was well known. She was family to Al and Rosa Hoots. Rosa was born in the territory, and she was half Osage.

Useeit got claimed that day after the race, a race she also got beaten in. A man came with a claim ticket, after the filly had been washed down and cooled out and readied for her stall.

He found himself looking down the wrong end of Mr Hoots' rifle, that man, and decided pretty quickly that maybe he could find another horse to buy. The stewards had to explain to Mr Hoots that sadly they would have to warn him off and remove Useeit from the Thoroughbred Register.

It was a long way home with Useeit, all the way back to Oklahoma.

Along the way, an idea came to him. He was excited to return home again. He was not well anymore. Upon his return, he announced to his wife that they were going to breed Useeit to a fine Thoroughbred stallion, and that, should anything happen to him, she was not on any account to sell the colt she was going to have, even though they didn't even really have money to cover her. She was going to be bred, and the resultant colt would win the Kentucky Derby.

He decided all this, just days after the filly he loved had been removed from the Thoroughbred Register.

Three things happened over the next couple of years. Al Hoots succumbed to his illness, and oil was discovered in Oklahoma, on Indian territory, meaning every Osage tribe member would gain an annual payment from the sale of the rights to that oil.

Rosa Hoots' share came to $12,000 a year. She was now able to write to the owner of successful Kentucky stallion Black Toney.

The third thing that happened was the Jockey Club relented and reinstalled Useeit into the Thoroughbred Register.

Useeit's foal by Black Toney was born in 1921 in Lexington, Kentucky. The colt was fine but small, and he was as dark as oil. And, since he maybe never would have been conceived without the money from those oil rights, Rosa named him Black Gold.

He ran his first race at Fair Grounds at the end of January of his 2-year-old year. The undeveloped young colt, still well shy of his actual second birthday, ran well enough. He ended up winning nine of his 17 races that year, including the Bashford Manor Stakes at Churchill Downs.

Shortly after, he began his partnership with jockey John David Mooney, known to everyone as JD. A young rider, born of Irish parents and raised in New Orleans ten minutes from the racetrack, he grew up riding the dray horses his father cared for.

The rider had held a covetous eye for the young black colt he would see regularly on the track in the mornings and raced against sometimes in the afternoons.

Black Gold matured and strengthened from two to three. He won the Louisiana Derby – then held at the Jefferson Racetrack. He had booked his ticket to head back to the state of his birth. He was going to run for The Roses.

In spite of his out-of-town credentials, and some condescension from connections of the more blue-blooded racing states, Black Gold went off favorite for the race. He lined up on the inside with 18 other 3-year-olds at the far end of the Churchill Downs straight, over 80,000 people there to witness. He met significant interference twice through the race, but it didn't matter. He still cut them down by the wire.

On May 17, 1924, Black Gold won the Kentucky Derby, in its golden jubilee year, the rider wearing the rose-colored silks of Mrs Hoots. He returned to the winner's enclosure and had that blanket of flowers placed over him. JD. picked one of the flowers and gave it to Rosa.

The black colt didn't go east for the Preakness or the Belmont Stakes afterwards. The trainer, Hanley Webb, went north with his single horse and won the Ohio State Derby and the Chicago Derby at Hawthorne. He won four derbies that year, but by its end his heavy campaign had taken its toll. He was sore, and the decision was taken to retire to stud the horse who won 18 from 35 starts and $111,000 in purses.

But then the oil well ran dry. He proved infertile. He produced only one foal in two seasons, and that single foal was struck by lightning and killed. The decision was made to return the sore horse to the track.

JD Mooney, his jockey, who had fallen in love with the young creature before he was ever actually united with him, was appalled and heartbroken and refused to be with the one he loved most.

Black Gold ran five times in his comeback, winning none of them. His final race was on January 18, 1928. The Salome Stakes at Fair Grounds. His ankle snapped in two places early in the home stretch, but the jockey could not pull him up. He hobbled on, past the wire.

Accounts differ, but it is of little matter. He was put down that day, after that race, five years after his first start at that very racetrack. They buried him in the infield, the brave little horse. A monument placed above him by the sixteenth pole is there to this day.

There were reports that Rosa Hoots ordered the horse returned to training as she had encountered financial difficulties. There were also rumors that she had taken out a $45,000 insurance policy on the horse. If those stories were true, then that last race was well named. Or was it the hard-pushing trainer, dismissive of the horse's plain calling of pain, who maybe was the real culprit.

The inaugural running of the Black Gold Stakes at Fair Grounds was held in 1958. The 2020 running is on Saturday (February 29). The winning rider traditionally places a wreath around that monument in the infield after the race, a touching way to keep alive, in some way, a piece of racing history.

There is one other horse buried next to Black Gold at Fair Grounds. Her name is Pan Zareta. She held the world record once as the fastest five-furlong sprinter. Useeit met her more than once. They raced against each other, eyeball to eyeball, when they were young and swift.

CHAPTER 12

The Life of a Young Jockey

Jack Gilligan, my son, has spent the past two winters racing at Fair Grounds in New Orleans, Louisiana. He spent his early years in Newmarket in England, where I trained a few horses. He started racing there, was apprenticed to Sir Mark Prescott. He was four from 26 in the UK, when he emigrated to the States, aged 17.

In one week, he went from early mornings mucking stables, tacking up, riding a few lots, sweeping the yard, to arriving at barns in Lexington, Kentucky, the horse tacked and pulled out for him. Up away, breeze, back in, and onto the next one. He hasn't mucked a stall or handled a broom since he arrived in the States over five years ago – and that suits him just fine.

Most jockeys in the UK will tell you about the driving, the traffic. Two meetings a day often, the M25, snarling tailbacks, time pressure. Seven days a week.

It must be a relief sometimes to get banned for a few days. It is tough to ride seven days a week. And it seems unnecessary to me, considering there is also jump racing running each day over there.

I didn't appreciate the pressure on a rider's shoulders when they are racing. It is intense – quick decisions, risk, getting it right. Time after time. No-one gets it right all the time, and that can weigh on the rider's mind.

A couple of days off gives the rider a chance to recharge, regroup. It is okay if a rider is winning all the time maybe, adrenaline is carrying them along, and nice paychecks. But most riders aren't winning all the time. I have seen the days off benefit Jack after a disappointing weekend.

Fair Grounds races four days a week through the winter, Thursday to Sunday, November through to the end of March. That is enough, he says. He likes the work-life balance here and the minimal driving. He lives a stone's throw from the track. Thirty-five minutes after his last race, he is showered and sat with his feet up at home.

Quite a difference from the UK – and to Jack here also when he races spring to autumn in Kentucky. Three-hour drives home after a disappointing day at the races is wearing. And they are mostly disappointing days, for everyone, everyone in the sport, loses more than they win.

We covered 72,000 miles the first year Jack rode in Kentucky. That is two and a half times around the circumference of the earth. He doesn't do that anymore, but riders in the UK don't have a choice, and, even if they have a driver, that is a lot of hours spent in a car.

Monday is quiet at Fair Grounds, a few morning breezers, go see some trainers, touch base with his agent, Richie 'The Rat' Price.

Jockey agents are much more hands-on with the riders here. They may have one rider on their book, no more than two. They charge the rider 25 percent of their weekly paycheck, and they go around the barns, see the trainers, hustle for new business, try to maintain existing business, and work on getting the rider as many winners as possible.

Riding fees and minor place percentages are low here. It is that ten percent of the winner's purse that the riders all want. Maiden races and allowance races here are running for around $46,000. Sixty percent of that goes to winning connections, and ten percent of that to the winning jockey, who then passes 25 percent to the agent and five percent to his valet.

Jockeys have to win here. A rider who has a dozen rides in a week without a winner in the UK is probably still making a living. Over here, a dozen rides and no win is McDonald's wages

Sunday and Monday is when Jack eats what he pleases. And in New Orleans, there is good eating to be had.

Sunday is Mid-City Pizza straight after racing, feet up, relax at home – he introduces me to a *Netflix* series, the *Haunting Of Hill House* – whatever you do, don't watch it. I never had the hair on my legs stand up before.

Monday, it may be Santa Fe, a big racing hangout around the corner from the track, or maybe Adolfo's down in the quaint and historic French Quarter. But there are so many. Drago's for seafood, Lola's for paella. Neyows for chargrilled oysters. And then there are the jazz bars and clubs dotted all over if you want to dance a few calories back off.

Almost every day, Jack takes a run in City Park or hits the gym. Weight is not easy for him here, even without so much temptation. He has to be able to ride, with his tack, at 118lb to stay competitive for mounts. That's 8 stone 6 pounds dressed, with his saddle. He is five feet nine inches, one of the three tallest riders in North America. So, after eating, well, comes the famine, literally. Tuesday and Wednesday, he doesn't eat really. A yoghurt and a protein bar and that is it both days.

I don't like it, but he says it's okay. It is the hardest part of his job, he says, but after two days he says he feels light and alert and good.

I flew down to see him, to spend a week with him. New Orleans is a great place to visit, a free spirited, laid-back city, mighty oaks draped with Spanish moss line the streets. You can happily spend an afternoon just wandering past the grand old homes, no cookie-cutter houses here. They are all shuttered windows and balconies and greens and pinks and blues, and it all works.

He had 13 rides booked over the weekend, which included a rare Monday card as it was Martin Luther King Day, a holiday. Three rides on the Thursday resulted in a close second, caught close home in the mile-and-an-eighth turf race.

We picked up some fish from Canseco's, the local store, after racing, walked home, realized it was frozen, so put it to defrost in the fridge and headed to Santa Fe around the corner for some Latin fusion food. There was a time when second was something to be excited about. Now it just sucks.

Friday, Jack was at the track breezing from 5.30 onwards. Jockeys don't get paid to breeze horses here, but they do expect to get the ride in the afternoon. So, it is good to be busy in the morning.

Straight after training, he went for a quick jog around City Park, then a shower and back to Fair Grounds. He likes to get to the track around two hours before his first race, to study his rides, to warm up and stretch and to share some banter with the jockeys and valets.

Two rides, races one and four, nothing to shout about. Straight in the shower and, like clockwork, he is back in the car 30 minutes after his last ride. We would have fish tonight, with broccoli and French stick. We went to the movies after, saw 1917. It was good, but I find war movies tough, all the wasted lives. We are lucky. I try harder as I get older to remind myself of that.

Saturday brought more breezes, I went to the track after the break, grabbed a coffee at CC's on the way and got some pictures of Jack breaking from the gate with Robby Albarado.

Home, shower, back to the races again. Three rides on the Saturday card, including **Silver Dust** in the Louisiana Stakes, a $100,000 Grade 3. Silver Dust provided Jack with his first two Graded Stakes last year. A difficult horse, he was rank to gallop, tough to breeze, and prone to rearing in the gate. At Saratoga, before Jack was associated with him, he reared over in the gate and got himself in such a tangle underneath the starting stalls that they had to be moved before he could get back up.

Jack had built up a good relationship with him, though, and the horse had talent. He would be favorite today, but this was his first start back after a break.

His first mount of the day didn't do much, neither did his second. It was turning into a quiet weekend. He looked well in the paddock, Silver Dust. He walked around like a prize fighter, the pale gray son of Tapit. He looked ready.

The jockeys came out in their silks, greeted the owners, talked to the trainers, then they were up and led out under the stands to the sound of the bugler.

Silver Dust warmed up well, kept on his leash by the pony rider. He loaded good, stood good. He broke fine from the inside stall, but three broke with him. Jack didn't want to lead – the horse can take it easy when he hits the front – but he didn't want to be pinned in by the other riders either. Silver Dust is tough, though, big and mean if he needs to be. Jack let him bully his way out as they came out of the first turn. Second now, just to the outside of the leader. Perfect. Now it was just a question of if he was good enough.

He was good enough. He joined the leader entering the stretch and drew away, they couldn't touch him today, a streak of gray, the rider's black and red silks laid along him, the stick flashed, keeping the old warrior to his task.

They came back to the winner's enclosure, the trainer relieved at a good job done, everyone smiling, laughing. Mission accomplished. It all went right, it all went good. It has to, to win. He might be better than ever this year, *Dusty*.

Margaritas at Santa Fe was the order of business after racing, dinner with Jack's friends. I drank too much, he was sensible. That is usually how it is in our family. We went down to Frenchmen Street afterwards, listened to some jazz bands in some dimly lit bars.

By the time I woke up the next day, Jack was already at the track. He came back during the break, picked me up and we headed to Bret Calhoun's barn to feed Silver Dust his mints. He took them as his due, ears pinned back by way of thank you. He was born April first, the same day my best horse was born, Rushcutter Bay. He is a grouch too, even now at age 27.

Sunday yielded a third, Monday was two unplaced runners followed by Mid-City Pizza again, Jack's treat to himself.

Stakes winners are a big deal to a young rider. Graded Stakes victories are not easy to come by. He has picked up three in the last 12 months, a sign of good progress for the rider, still only 23, already over 300 wins to his name.

He has worked hard since he left school, and indeed rode out every day before school since the age of 14. He is reaping some rewards now. He drives his big truck, has just bought a nice condo here in

New Orleans. The living is good down here in the Big Easy, for the kid from Newmarket in the UK. Who would have written that?

Just three days after leaving New Orleans, I was back – to visit Jack in hospital.

It was the last race on the Friday, problems on the last turn, a horse swung out, knocked Jack's mount off balance and it went down.

I was watching the race at home in Lexington. One second it was a normal race, the next everything had changed. It was faster than the human eye could see – he just disappeared from the screen, a horrible fast fall, fired into the ground. His collarbone instantly snapped.

A horse and rider from behind couldn't avoid them, the animal tried to jump the horse on the ground, half made it, but its foot struck Jack in the face as it galloped by. The rider returned devastated, scared. It broke Jack's eye sockets, his nose. They will have to operate to realign his jaw. Wires for six weeks, no solids.

You wouldn't normally consider that lucky, but everything shall mend, full movement except in that left arm. Not in extreme pain. Six weeks out though, possibly on the sidelines for Silver Dust's next race. That may be the worst pain of all.

I wonder if Shaun Bridgmohan, the other rider downed, when he was flying through the air a seeming good dozen feet off the ground at over 30 miles an hour with his horse no longer beneath him, had pause to reconsider his career choice. Probably not. Jack is already starting to grumble about missed mounts. It takes years off you, days like this.

CHAPTER 13

Luca Cumani

I had never really spoken to Luca Cumani until I was leaving Newmarket to come to the States. He came with his son Matt to view our house and stables. By the end of the meeting I found a personal warmth in him, maybe a hint of melancholy, I don't know, but he has something. By the end of the viewing his son Matt had nearly convinced me that I should give him money to take our yard, I thought then he might do well, and that he had obviously been well trained...

Luca Cumani was born the son of a top Italian trainer, a dashing amateur rider, he won the Fegentri championship in 1972. He came to Newmarket and was assistant to Henry Cecil from 1973 -75. He captured the most beautiful woman in town in her day and made her his wife and quite frankly he has seemed pretty pleased with himself ever since.

He won two Epsom Derby's with Kahyasi and High Rise and the Breeders Cup Mile with Barathea. Perhaps though, his own performance as a sire may end up being a significant contribution to racing itself. Francesca his daughter who inherited her mother's beauty and yet seems disarmingly unaware of it, is a face of horse racing in the UK and Australia, and her brother Matt eventually decided to set up as a trainer down under also, and is rapidly rising through the ranks.

I only really have to say Italian, to describe Luca Cumani. Slim, brooding, olive skin, dark eyes and a curiously beguiling voice, a mix of Italian, immaculate English, and a lifetime of five star hotels.

Luca Cumani has won too much to list, and mentored too many to count, Frankie Dettori was his stable apprentice for god's sake. He has dry wit and a sharp mind and I think he misses his son.

Who Do You Think Is The Most Important Person In World Racing History?

Well, being Italian, I would have to say Federico Tesio. What he achieved as a breeder owner and trainer has been unmatched and will be unmatched possibly forever, it was unbelievable what he did. Winning big races all over Europe in a time when transport wasn't easy. He won at Goodwood and Ascot and France and all over Europe.

What Is Your Favorite Race And Venue?

That is a tricky one, as there are so many. I would have to say Goodwood in the UK for its scenery, Santa Anita in the States, again for its scenery and in Australia it's Melbourne for its atmosphere.

My favorite race I would have to say is the Juddmonte International, I was lucky enough to win it three times, (Commanche Run, One So Wonderful and Falbrav) and it's probably one of the best races in the world. As we have seen over the last few years it often seems to produce the highest rated performance in the world. I think it's a great race on a very fair track, it's a typical mid-season, summer season race, usually run on good ground over a distance that suits most horses. So I think it's the best race in the world.

What is your Fondest Memory in Racing?

Well it has to be Barathea winning the Breeders Cup. I had a lot of emotional attachment through Gerald Leigh who bred the horse and was still a part-owner of the horse and he was there so it was very emotional. Gerald Leigh was a friend of mine for many many years, and a great supporter of our stable so Barathea winning that race was an enormous pleasure.

What Do You See As The Biggest Problem Racing Faces Today?

It has to be welfare because unfortunately the vast majority of people outside racing don't really understand racing and don't really understand the amount of passion and love that goes into the care of the horses and I think it is a big challenge for us in racing, to keep educating people, showing them how we look after these horses and care for them. And we can do more and must do more around the world, we must keep working at it to allay this false perception.

If You Could Change One Thing In Racing What Would It Be?

When it comes to English racing we know what the problem is, it's a lack of prize money, So if I could change anything I would like to have a structure whereby racing has control of its finances which it hasn't at the moment.

The British Horseracing Authority does a great job but it doesn't cover the commercial side of racing, it only covers governance and regulation so there is not a body in England that looks after the financial structure and therefore the commercial interests of racing and so much more could be done in order to bring in more money.

Racing in England is such a superb spectacle but it's only thanks to the many patrons we do have, from the Queen to our friends in the Middle East that we have the best racing, and we do have the best racing in the world, but we need to incentivize owners through prize money.

CHAPTER 14

The Cheltenham Festival

The Cheltenham Festival starts on Tuesday. The most ferocious four days in racing there is. Steeplechasing's Breeders Cup. When the tape goes up and the runners set off for the first race on the first day, there will be a roar that shakes the surrounding hills.

Imagine if every big race of the Saratoga meet was squeezed into four days. Imagine if all those fans of Saratoga, all those people in love with the place, had only four days to savor it, to breath it in, to experience it, imagine if all those great Saratoga horses were all there for only four days.

It is too much really, an assault on the senses, 50,000 spectators, every one of them there to watch horses and to bet like they don't have a wife or family.

Fortunes are bet, individual wagers in excess of £100,000 are recorded. The Irish come over like an invading army, to take on the old enemy, seeking reparations from when the English came and overstayed their welcome (they seemed to do a lot of that). The Irish make the festival, there for the *craic*, there for the horses, there for the stout.

An Irishman one year claimed he won enough on the first day to clear his mortgage. On the third day he lost his house. "It was only a small house," he said.

The horses, beautiful, big, gallant, strong. I've jumped steeplechase fences on those horses. It was the best feeling in the world back then. You will never know how strong a racehorse really is until you fly over a big fence at speed, when they launch. It is a game for young men, though, young men made of steel and coated in titanium. There are some young women doing it now, as good as the best men. They are made of steel too and coated in titanium.

John Francome, legendary ex-steeplechase rider, was asked by a reporter once if he ever missed it. "Miss it?" He said. "I can't believe I was ever bloody daft enough to do it in the first place."

It is crazy, and crazily dangerous too, but beautiful and poetic at the same time. Such a spectacle.

The horses return tired, exhausted, three miles, 20-plus fences, carrying over 160 pounds often. It seems cruel maybe. Maybe it is cruel. Life is cruel. But these warriors, if they aren't taken by injury, return year after year, they are loved and become friends, heroes. The best of them have their exploits detailed on the national news.

Four days, full Irish breakfast, to the races, read the form, look at the horses, bet. Repeat seven times. Leave the racecourse, head to a country pub, sit by the fire with a hot toddy, eat steak, talk about today's racing and tomorrow's over more drinks, go to bed. Repeat for four days, then go home and don't look at another horse race for at least a week.

You can't. It is too pale, too wan, after what you have just experienced.

CHAPTER 15

Omaha Beach

He did it easy, Omaha Beach. A romp, his bowling stride too much for the others. The ante-post Kentucky Derby favorite, the last-minute scratch due to a breathing problem. Surgery performed successfully. A win, a second, and then victory in the G1 Malibu One more run, then retirement from the racetrack beckons, and a career as a stallion begins, for the horse who might have won the Roses.

He is well named, Omaha Beach, being by War Front. Omaha Beach was one of the landing beaches of the allied forces on the D Day landings in France on June 6, 1944. The others were Utah, Gold, Juno and Sword. Omaha was the deadliest landing beach. Heavy German artillery guns in concrete bunkers are still there on the beach. Two and a half thousand Americans died on that beach. Young men, who fought for our freedom.

Omaha Beach was just down the road. We had a friend, an owner, who holidayed with us. He was a lifelong serviceman in the British military. He wanted to visit Omaha, so we all went.

We went and saw those giant concrete bunkers with those giant guns, we went to the museum, and learned about the landings. We learned it was a bloody mess. Strong weather and currents took care of many members of the two infantry divisions while attempting to land, tanks sank – with their crews. Water up to the soldiers necks, strong currents. And then they faced the strafing German machine guns.

We learned about all the casualties. But those two infantry divisions took that beach. We couldn't imagine it, here on a sunny day, people wandering, eating ice cream, talking, relaxed, we couldn't visualize it, what happened right there on that beach, back then.

We visited the American Cemetery afterwards. It was the most beautiful terrible thing we had ever seen. Row upon row upon row of white crosses. It is the quietest place I have ever been to.

We wandered past all the crosses in silence, saw all the names. No-one was eating ice cream here. No-one was talking.

It is hard to visualize war. But come here, and see the 10,000 white crosses, the whole place immaculate, the grass pristine, the silence stilling you. There is a giant monument beside a large square pond. There are 1,500 names on The Walls of the Missing there. Never found, nothing left of them.

Operation Pegasus took place a few months after the D Day landings. It was a rescue mission that successfully evacuated 138 allied soldiers stranded in German occupied territory.

Omaha Beach maybe rescued Santa Anita a bit on Sunday. So, it is fitting maybe that the Pegasus World Cup shall be his next and final race.

I hope Omaha Beach is a success at stud, I hope his name shall live on, so people don't forget. I had forgotten until I went there. I won't forget now. We all forget sometimes, don't we, how lucky we really are?

CHAPTER 16

Old Abe

There were two famous men known as old Abe in the mid-19th century. One of them had the last name Lincoln. The other, for much of his life, had no last name. He was the most celebrated jockey in the land in his day. A man born a slave, sold along with the horses he rode, his history guessed at, half a name, traded as livestock. But astride a horse, he was a prince.

We don't know who his parents were, or for sure where he was from, though Mississippi is touted, or even whether he was traded or sold before Duncan Kenner, the owner of Ashland Plantation in Louisiana, purchased him for $2,300 in 1854.

The sale was listed in the papers of the time, along with other bloodstock bought and sold.

It was a considerable sum, but he was already by then known as a considerable rider. The arrangement by which he was allowed to ride races and travel to meets is unknown. The picture accompanying this piece is the only known image of a jockey who became famous from south to north to east of the vast semi-tamed continent of North America.

He was a small man, only the size of a child, and he had a speech impediment, which may have contributed to his silent manner. But he could talk with horses. He became known as 'The Black Prince' and 'The Dark Sage of Louisiana'.

The notorious Whale, an unbeaten racer but a horse no other man dared touch or try to handle, much less ride, would stand still under old Abe, until the rider closed his heels on him. Then he would spring to life and race, with Abe buried in his mane, sat forward and out of the saddle, maybe the first to do so. Which makes him perhaps, the father of all modern day jockeys.

The Civil War made him a free man. He went north to Saratoga a year later, took the last name Hawkins, and was famous before he arrived. He won the third running of the Travers in 1866, on Merrill, a horse trained by another ex-slave, Ansel Williamson – the man who just under a decade later would train Aristides to win the very first Kentucky Derby.

In a time when race results did not regularly include the riders name, old Abe's would often be found beside his mounts' names, whether they won or not.

He made money and saved it. He seems to have been a man of modest appetites. A lifetime of rationed basic food probably stayed with him. There is no record of a wife or children, his parents are unknown.

His quiet manner probably left him lonely. With his stutter, lack of education and slight bearing, he probably found it easier being around horses. Maybe he was drawn to them for this reason. Many people who carry pain within them find solace in those big noble creatures. Perhaps they were the only other slaves he spent time with.

He whipped those slaves for their white masters, and it made him famous and rich. We don't know if it made him happy.

Kenner lost his 500 slaves in the Civil War, and with it his wealth, temporarily. It is said that old Abe sent word to Kenner that he would help him if financial assistance was sought.

Who knows if that happened? What we do know is that, when Abe became sick with the tuberculosis that would take him, he returned to the Ashland plantation where he was raised a slave. It is said Kenner tended to him as a parent to a child, and, after his death in 1867, he was buried not in the slave cemetery but in a brick tomb under a mighty oak overlooking the training track of Ashland.

Did he return to Ashland as a son returns home though, in need? No, he returned to Ashland because the place he was a slave was the only home he knew, his master and fellow slaves the only people he had ties with.

What was freedom to a man, born a slave, taken from his parents, allowed no possessions, given no choices, no education, no rights? What was freedom really to a man, already older and sick, probably scared and tired and unable to convey his own feelings and thoughts, inarticulate, except when astride the mighty beasts? Only then did the Black Prince have something to say to the world. Then he was bigger than other men, then other men cheered him, and sang his name, and he lived in the pages of the newspapers and telegraphs. But, once he stepped off the animal, he slipped once again, into the shadows.

He was lucky, to have died in some comfort, some care taken off his carcass, some memory of him to live on. Most slaves didn't experience that. I doubt if Kenner made such fuss of his 500 other slaves.

I don't really know what the morality of owning other animals is. Perhaps future generations will judge us harshly, breeding these animals for our sport. I do know that is why we have a moral duty towards these animals, raised in captivity by us, fed by us at our leisure, forced to labor for us. Sold and traded by us.

Many experts think now that horses, to a lesser or greater degree, possess probably the same six basic primary emotions we feel – fear, disgust, anger, happiness, sadness and surprise – and that they are adroit in recognizing those same emotions in us. If they have the same feelings as us, the same emotions, then our moral duty to their well-being is high while we put them to work for our purposes.

Old Abe and Whale, bound together, slaves together, talking together as they thundered down the track, whispering in the wind, shaking a fist to the world in those moments. Angry Whale, and quiet, sad, old Abe.

CHAPTER 17
Sunshine

It takes up to 100,000 years for a photon to travel from the sun's core where it is created, to the sun's outer surface, and then a further eight minutes to travel the 99 million miles to Earth.

Only a small amount (ten percent) of the ultraviolet (UVB) radiation photons will make it through the atmosphere, the ozone layer capturing the rest, heating the atmosphere and stopping us all being fried.

The light that makes it through coats the planet and every living creature walking on it. When it hits the skin of a horse (or human) it reacts with cholesterol in the skin and produces cholecalciferol (pre-vitamin D3). This is then synthesized by the liver to produce calcifediol, which then travels to the kidneys and is converted to calcitriol, an active form of D3.

Vitamin D3 – the sunshine vitamin – is important because it regulates calcium and phosphorus uptake. And that is important, because it is well known that calcium is utilized for strong bones.

If vitamin D3 is synthesized from UVB light from the sun, though, where does that leave young racehorses who are stabled 24/7, often exercised in the dark, or early morning when UV light is weak, and even if trained late in the morning, are not out long enough to absorb sufficient sunlight to synthesize necessary levels of D3?

Around 40 percent of Americans have mild vitamin D deficiency. A chronic deficiency causes rickets with weak, poorly developed bowed and deformed limbs. This was treated and virtually eradicated with oral supplementation of D3 rich cod-liver oil in the early 20th century.

The literature on vitamin D3 is limited and sometimes contradictory where equines are concerned.

Some studies suggest vitamin D deficiency could be common, some say it is rare, but since it is reckoned that a horse would require somewhere between two and eight hours in a field depending on weather and if rugged, and whether the horse is young and growing (an 18-month-old growing young horse could require up to 90 percent more vitamin D than a mature animal) to obtain all its vitamin D requirements, it is obvious that the young racehorse shall not obtain its D3 requirements in the way nature intended.

In the absence of turnout, oral supplementation seems to be effective, and indeed most, though not all feed companies, list added vitamin D levels in their nutritional analysis. Hay and alfalfa contain highly variable levels of vitamin D2, depending on how it is prepared and its age, and modern farming methods may have a negative impact on levels. Also vitamin D2 is perhaps not processed by the body as efficiently as D3.

While oral supplementation of vitamin D3 is effective, it is thought that it does not provide the same bone strength as vitamin D3 synthesized naturally, and excessive oral over-supplementation can result in toxicosis, which can lead to calcification of organs and even death in very extreme cases. This does not happen when synthesized naturally through the skin as, when the animal has produced enough D3, it begins to synthesize other sterols.

In addition to vitamin D deficiency resulting in bone weakness, leading to possible increased predisposal to fractures, as well as poorer joint health, including physitis and increased risk of stress fractures and sore shins, it is linked to other conditions in the horse, with lesser or more degrees of certainty – ulcers, Inflammatory Airway Disease, exertional rhabdomyolysis, gait stiffness, appetite suppression, depression, loss of condition, immune suppression, poor muscle contraction.

I have found no research linking vitamin D deficiency, or lack of natural D3 production, playing some role in bone bruising, but it would be logical to consider it may be a potential factor.

Anyone who has ever worked in a Thoroughbred stable knows these conditions are many of the most common problems affecting young Thoroughbreds in training.

We know for certain that nearly all young Thoroughbreds in training, who do not have daily turnout, must be naturally deficient in vitamin D3. Oral supplementation is effective for most equines, but in the case of a young racehorse undergoing intense training, oral supplementation may prove inadequate.

Wolff's law states that bone remodels according to the stresses placed upon it. No horse's bones are stressed more than a young Thoroughbred's in training, yet it has been suggested that a lack of adequate daily sunlight – even with oral supplementation – produces an animal with poorer bone integrity.

With the myriad other conditions possibly linked to vitamin D deficiency, and indeed toxicity, this may be an area where further research could be strongly indicated.

Perhaps the use of UV lamps, to improve absorption through the skin, allowing endogenous synthesis of vitamin D3 naturally, could improve bone density in young racehorses in training. I am not aware of any studies that have addressed this, but in humans UV lamps have been shown to raise circulating vitamin D3 levels. It may, however, just be Wolff's law again, horses outside run about more than stabled horses, stressing their bones in multiple ways, thus strengthening them.

In the winter of 2018-19, I was overseeing a string of horses at Payson Park in Florida. There was a 2-year-old filly, turning three. Twice she had been taken out of training. She would get too tight, too stiff to train. We stopped with her and turned her out daily for several hours.

In Europe we call it *Doctor Grass* and prescribe paddock turnout for horses who are sore, off their feed, have ulcers, or for horses who have just trained off, and for many other reasons, including just a holiday.

After a few weeks, when she started bucking and kicking again and running around the paddock, I put her back in training, starting her off with a small amount of phenylbutazone daily to hopefully keep her feeling good.

She went through her exercise regime fine this time around and ended up winning her maiden special weight at Keeneland in the spring. At the time, I put her improvement down to rest, grass, phenylbutazone, and further maturity. Maybe though, Professor Sunshine had just been looking down and smiling on us all along.

There are a couple of points to bear in mind here for humans also. Studies on jockeys have shown, rather surprisingly, that they demonstrated relatively poor bone density. Cholesterol is a fat. Without its presence in the skin, vitamin D3 cannot be produced through exposure to sunlight. My son recently took part in a fitness assessment of jockeys at the University of Kentucky. He had the lowest body fat they had measured at 4.5%, (athletes average 6-14%, average male 18-25%). Jockeys may need to monitor their D3 levels too.

Finally, optimal vitamin D levels have been shown in studies to be protective in humans against many illnesses, including cold and influenza virus. There are also preliminary reports of vitamin D deficiency possibly being related to higher mortality rates in Covid-19 cases.

So a bit of sunshine may be beneficial for both horses and humans at this time.

CHAPTER 18

Flat Earth Society

The first official record of a racecourse in North America was one laid out on Hempstead Plains on Long Island by Colonel Richard Nicholls, the man who in 1664 took New Amsterdam from the Dutch settlers there, and, on behalf of the British Crown, renamed the place New York.

The course laid out on that plain would have been similar to the many expansive sweeping racecourses in the old land. He even named it Newmarket. Why wouldn't he? That is what horse racing was, gentlemen pitting their horses against each other, mostly in matches, from point to point, often run in heats, at distances of up to four miles across heathland, or downland.

When racing horses took off in Virginia, tobacco fields that had become infertile were used to mark out a circular course. People came to watch the races. People loved to come and watch the races.Then, as right now, it was the only sport in town.

Racing carried on like this on the turf, more and more often around fields in a circle of sorts, and over time a circumference of a mile grew common.

For much of this time, the eastern half of the USA was a vast 1,000-mile high and 1,000-mile wide forest, thick with trees. Some of those ancient trunks measured 15 feet across. It must have been backbreaking, heartbreaking work clearing those million square miles.

I took down a tree with just an axe in my youth, a puny thing in someone's driveway. I still remember those roots. So, the strip of land cleared down that eastern coast was precious – and not for two- or four-mile-long racecourses.

The Newmarket racecourse, though, was still in use when the Union Course was set out in New York in 1821 in an oval, and, for the first time recorded, for some reason they raced on a skinned track. It was North America's, and indeed the world's, first dirt racetrack.

Horses, it was said, ran two to three seconds faster on the new dirt track than the old grass track of Newmarket. And right from the beginning, it was noted that innumerable horses were lamed on such tracks.

The desire for speed measured by stopwatch, perhaps fueled by the evolution of such watches (Kentucky watches, they were sometimes called) prevailed over concerns for safety in a wild and unsafe world. Early speed was an advantage. Pace and toughness were required, and the adoption of dirt may even have been to cock a snoot to the recently vanquished powers of the old world, putting an American stamp on a sport of the British aristocracy.

A more democratic sport, a sport any man could come and watch, the oval mile making for easy viewing by all.

And now, almost exactly 200 years later, it is still the preferred racing surface in the U.S., many race fans unaware that Americans raced solely on turf for 150 years.

Turf racing largely disappeared from U.S. racing but is experiencing a resurgence now. I think it would be great to see a Turf Triple Crown married to the dirt one. Same races, same days. One turf, one dirt.

The forests are gone now – America is vast and open – but the ubiquitous dirt oval is entrenched in horsemen's minds here. It seems a shame. One of the nicest places to go racing in the States is Kentucky Downs, a small five-day meet that races around a nine-furlong undulating grass course. Big fields, big money, big name riders and trainers.

I know I'm a European, used to racing on turf, and in later years synthetic tracks, and that in Europe the importance of times – an interesting and very educational aspect of U.S. racing – doesn't hold the same fascination. "Time only matters if you're in prison" is the dismissive (and wrong) consensus of some European trainers.

I don't know what to predict for horse racing in the U.S., for dirt racing, what will win out. Safety and modernization – or the prising of that last handful of dirt out of the sport's dying fist.

Horse racing is a great sport here. I, like most European racing fans, love watching the Breeders' Cup each year. But will it eventually be buried by public opinion? The Covid crisis saved American racing from being in the newspapers for all the wrong reasons once again after the doping arrests, which came so quickly after the disaster that was Santa Anita.

Stay quiet, change nothing, ignore the critics. Not having a governing body that is accountable means no one has to answer to the public. Put a band-aid on it. Another year another thousand dead horses. Americans are known as innovators, they created the first artificial racetracks – they just never updated them.

If the U.S. motor industry was as innovative as the U.S. horse racing industry, your car would still have ears.

I know it irritates some people when I talk about safety. Progress is often unpopular until, with the benefit of hindsight, people admit that progress was necessary.

Should voting rights for women be rescinded? Should higher education be only for the wealthy? Should smoking be allowed again in planes and movie theaters and restaurants? Should seatbelts and airbags be removed?

Someday U.S. racing will abolish race-day medications and find a safer surface that sits better with the U.S. horsemen. Either that or someday the public will likely send horse racing the way of greyhound racing.

U.S. racing didn't use to race on dirt, and it didn't use to race on drugs. Now it does both and the people stopped watching. They turned away. Is it possible to make U.S. racing widely popular and great again?

With the stance of the Kentucky Horsemen's Benevolent and Protective Association (KHBPA) opposing the Kentucky Horse Racing Commission's (KHRC) decision to ban lasix in 2-year-old races this year, no chance. They make the Flat Earth Society appear enlightened and progressive in comparison.

Jason Servis et al have pled not guilty to the charges made against them. That raises the prospect of those transcripts, discussing horses killed and drugged, making headlines, quite possibly around the world, if the cases go to trial.

American racing might not just bring itself down, it could strike a blow against the sport globally, tarnish its reputation even in the majority of countries where horsemen take seriously their duty of care towards their horses and riders.

A national governing body is urgently needed here. Kentucky maybe needs horse racing. California certainly doesn't, and neither does New York. Neither do most states.

The rest of the racing world may need to distance themselves from U.S. racing if this case blows up internationally in the media. How shall U.S. racing defend itself when it makes no serious progress, when the horsemen are seen fighting against every genuine effort to clean up their own house? By producing PR stunts and skirting around the major issues. I genuinely don't understand why.

Horsemen never want change. Back in the UK, we would have our trainers' meetings and grumble about every new change the British Horseracing Authority was going to introduce. And then, after those changes were implemented, we would accept it, and get on with grumbling about the next change.

Nearly all those changes were progressive and better for the horses and riders and public perception, and the sport grew in popularity and prestige year on year.

It is just Lasix. Race without it, in 2-year olds. Try it for a year. See if the planet stops turning. But they need it for racing on dirt, they say. Well, there lies the answer, doesn't it?

If you need to drink alcohol to treat your alcoholism, people on the outside looking in might think you are going about things the wrong way.

I'm not suggesting America does something impossible – like land a man on the moon. I'm just suggesting that maybe NYRA, CHRB,

KHRC, etc could get together and agree on common-sense, unified rules and penalties that send a clear message to all participants that training racehorses is a privilege, not a right.

CHAPTER 19

Steve Cauthen

I have been in Kentucky for six years now. I know the Kentucky accent. It can be slightly whiny, drawn out, at times even a little irritating. Steve Cauthen was born and raised in Kentucky, but, when he speaks, women everywhere start swooning, It was always like that. I sat down with him recently and listened to him talk.

"My dad was born in Texas, a little town called Muleshoe. He carried a pistol to school. That's how it was back then in Texas. He left to go to the racetrack at 16. He was a groom, exercise rider, he trained some, then at some point he went to blacksmith school and became a farrier."

Cauthen's family on his maternal side had a successful butter-producing company and owned racehorses. His first winner was trained by his mother's brother.

"I loved sports, loved football. When I was ten or 11, I wanted to be a quarterback, but then all my buddies grew up and I didn't. Then I read a book, *I Ride to Win* by Eddie Arcaro, and that piqued my interest."

Cauthen had been riding since the age of two, so he approached his father and told him he would like to try to become a jockey. Instead of clipping him around the ear like a good father would, Tex said sure, that he would help him in any way he could.

From the age of 15, Cauthen was sneaked onto the backstretch at River Downs racetrack in Ohio to exercise horses and, as soon as he turned 16, he approached the senior steward to ask to take out his jockey's license. "I looked about ten and was skinny as a rake. He said, 'I think we need to think about this.'"

After being vouched for by other racetrackers, Cauthen's license was obtained, and it wasn't long before he donned silks. His first ride finished just about last, and he rode a few more slow ones before he rode that first winner for his uncle. He rode another the next day, for his mother on a horse raised at the family farm.

Cauthen won three races on the bounce, and he was off. He ended up riding over a hundred winners at River Downs over the next couple of months.

"Then I went to Chicago, to Arlington Park. They were already halfway through the meet, but I finished runner-up in the standings there." The young kid from Kentucky managed to rack up 240 winners in 1976, the first year he rode races.

He was just getting going, though. He was in New York for the winter and had top agent Lenny Goodman now. He was unstoppable.

No one had ever seen anything like it.

In 1977, Steve Cauthen rode over 2,000 races and won 487 of them. His mounts earned over $6 million that year, which netted the 17-year-old somewhere around $600,ooo before deductions. The median price of a home in Kentucky at that time was a little under $60,000.

Cauthen was champion apprentice in 1977, and also champion jockey, and he won the Eclipse award of merit for the person who did the most for horse racing that year.

Perhaps the most important thing that happened that year, though, was Cauthen picking up a spare mount in a 2-year-old stakes at Saratoga on a horse called Affirmed. He won that race, and then followed up in the Hopewell Stakes against his soon-to-be-famous adversary, Alydar.

"That was the day I knew he was the real deal. I'd never accelerated that much on any horse before. They ran all the way from the quarter pole to the wire." The score stood Alydar one, Affirmed two. Perhaps the greatest series of duels in modern racing history was heating up.

"Then we won the Futurity, and then Alydar beat me in the Champagne Stakes [at Belmont Park]. It was a muddy track and Alydar came wide, Affirmed was never that comfortable on an off track."

The following year Affirmed and Cauthen won the Santa Anita Derby and the Hollywood Derby in California, and then they headed back to Kentucky, to Run for the Roses, to go head to head with Alydar once again.

I asked him how he had felt. Had he been nervous – riding a big mount in the biggest race in North America. "Hey, I was just happy to have my first ride in a classic race. I was excited, nervous, not worried about it."

Affirmed broke well, Alydar didn't. Cauthen found a spot on the outside in third, Alydar was wide and out of his ground. When Steve Cauthen unleashed Affirmed at the top of the stretch, it was as good as over. Alydar closed, he tried, but he couldn't make up all that ground. The kid won the Kentucky Derby on Affirmed. The horse stood in the winner's enclosure with the young rider in pink and black silks, and a blanket of red roses was laid across them. Alydar was second.

The Preakness Stakes at Pimlico in Maryland falls exactly two weeks after the Kentucky Derby. Affirmed was there. So was Alydar. The result was the same, Affirmed first, but only by a neck this time, and a lot of people thought the mile and a half at Belmont Park would suit Alydar better. He had already beaten Affirmed twice at Belmont Park. The bettors made him favorite to do it again.

"Now that was a long three weeks leading up to the Belmont. If I was ever nervous in my whole life it was kind of leading up to the Belmont because I knew I had a chance to do something really special and was young and I didn't want to be the reason it got screwed up."

Affirmed cruised to an easy lead in the Belmont. A half-mile in 50 was slow for horses of their calibre. Jorge Velasquez on Alydar decided to duel, to lay it down to Affirmed, to make his lungs burn, to test his stamina, to test his heart.

They joined together, eyeball to eyeball, still three quarters of a mile from the winning post. The pair went clear. It was just them, Affirmed on the inner, Alydar laying down on him. They jousted down the stretch, and Alydar got a head up. And Cauthen switched his stick and asked Affirmed for more. He fought back, closed inch by inch, both riders reaching deep into their horses' souls. Both horses fought, and they flashed by the wire together. And 18-year-old Steve Cauthen and 3-year-old Affirmed had won the Triple Crown.

He was famous across North America now, Cauthen, the winner of one of the greatest duels in the sport, winner of the Triple Crown. He was featured in *Sports Illustrated*, more than a jockey, a face of the times, featured on the cover of *Time* magazine, named *Sports Illustrated Sportsman of the Year* – the only jockey ever to win the accolade. All against the backdrop of flared jeans and the Bee Gees. It seemed too good to be true. And it was.

An injury ruled him off Affirmed in the Travers. The horse still passed the post in front but was disqualified for interference, handing the win to Alydar.

When Cauthen retook the mount, they got beaten a few races in succession. People murmured about Cauthen's fitness, whether his injury was still bothering him. He didn't think it did, but that didn't stop them taking him off his horse. The horse he won the Triple Crown on was no longer his to ride.

And then people decided the kid had forgotten how to ride. He was out in California, and a quiet spell turned into a drought. "The press wrote each day how long it had been since my last winner and how many mounts."

That was an asinine thing to do to the teenager, still not even old enough yet to buy a brew to wash the bad taste out of his mouth. They say the higher you climb, the farther you fall. Well Steve Cauthen was tumbling from the stars. And it stung. Of course it stung.

But then came a racehorse owner from England, the champion racehorse owner in England. He had noted the young man, was impressed by his politeness when he came across him in California once. He got bloodstock agent Billy McDonald to ask the kid who had grown from five foot one to five foot six by now, and was filling his frame, whether he might consider Europe.

The young rider demurred at first, so Robert Sangster paid him a visit. He sat with Steve and Tex, convinced them that, with his height, he would have to head there sometime for the higher weights, so why not now? Tex gave his blessing, and the Kentucky Kid packed his bags and got on a plane and left everything he had achieved behind.

"I flew into Ireland, and then they snuck me over to Blackbushe airport in Camberley, Surrey, so nobody would know I was coming in. So, I meet [trainer] Barry [Hills] with his car, and I say 'Hi Barry, nice to meet you, shall I put my case in your trunk? And he says, 'It's called an f-ing boot here.'"

And the young man suddenly realized his home state of old-fashioned southern manners was now far behind him.

I asked him what he remembers of those first days in England. "I remember riding two miles to the gallop and four miles home in the rain and wind and cold," he smiles.

"Barry and Penny were great. They put me up in their house until I eventually got my own place. They became like parents to me and treated me like family from the beginning. Barry was a big influence on me. He reignited my desire to be on top again."

Cauthen won on his first mount in the UK – for Barry Hills – and he was just as instantly successful at disarming the British press – in fact, pretty much the whole racing community. He had immaculate manners, a complete lack of self-importance, and level-headed openness and honesty. He was so honest in fact that, when a trainer one day instructed him to ride his horse like a non-trier, he had to ask what a non-trier was.

Just a month after meeting Barry Hills, the pair of them won the 2000 Guineas with Tap On Wood "I think I won about six Group races in the first six weeks we were there, and then the horses got sick. That's when I learned to play golf. I ended up having about 50-odd winners that season."

"I loved being with Barry and Penny. He was a very good trainer, a self-made man, and maybe he didn't get all the credit he deserved."

They went racing together. Cauthen recalls a hairy drive to Nottingham one day, when they entrusted him to drive their big new

Mercedes. They were together for six years, but then Henry Cecil made him an offer. One his head had to accept, although with some sadness as it meant his time with Hill's was to end.

Slip Anchor was there, that first year. "After he won the Lingfield Derby [Trial], I called my dad and said I wanted him to come over. I thought we could win the Derby."

He did win the Epsom Derby on Slip Anchor, seven years after winning the Kentucky one, still the only man to do so. Then a few days later he won the Oaks on Oh So Sharp.

He says without hesitation that Oh So Sharp was the best he rode in Europe. She became his second Triple Crown winner. They won four of the five English Classics, the first year Cecil and Cauthen teamed up.

I asked him what he made of Newmarket when he first got there. "It was cool, but it got me drinking ... by the end of the year I was in a drying out joint," he says chuckling (he is teetotal now).

I asked him who he thought were the best, toughest competitors on either side of the Atlantic. "Angel Cordero in the States was tough, always looking for a way to get your horse beat." And in Europe he mentioned Lester Piggott of course, and also Pat Eddery. "Pat was a natural. He couldn't tell you how he did it, but he just knew how to do it."

He spent six years with Cecil, "I loved riding for Henry. He was eccentric for sure, but there was something about him. He was special." They were both special, and they were special years, Cecil in his prime, a glamorous pairing, picking up prestige races all over the place. There was another Derby with Reference Point. And Cauthen won the Irish, French and Italian Derbies too.

And then in 1990 Sheikh Mohammed made him an offer he couldn't refuse. He won two G1s for Andre Fabre in France, including one on Rose Finch, a daughter of Oh So Sharp, during his two years with the Sheikh.

He climbed the two tallest mountains in the sport, Steve Cauthen. He stood on those peaks, breathed in the air and took in the view. And then, at the age of 32, he decided to stop climbing. He stopped racing horses for fortune and fame, laid down his champagne glass, and he took his young wife, Amy, carrying the first of their three daughters, and returned to Kentucky – the 'land of meadows' in the Iroquois language.

Kentucky is a beautiful state, with four beautiful seasons, and Cauthen raised his family there on his farm. He raised horses too, he still does, and he owns some and manages some. He is laid back and friendly, living here in this laid back and friendly state.

Cauthen would have made a lot of money riding horses, but money can be made in many ways. When he sits at home in his armchair, though, and rests his head back and closes his eyes, he can be behind Affirmed's ears once again, thundering down the stretch, under the Twin Spires, reaching for the wire in the 104th Kentucky Derby. Or he can have Oh So Sharp, in his hands, cruising around Tattenham Corner, before unleashing her in the Oaks.

Before he left, he said he wanted to ask me a favour. "I'd like it if you could say something nice about Barry, Penny, and Pat. I thought very highly of them, I thought they were all great."

They were great, Barry Hills with his cigars, Pat Eddery with his large blue eyes. Icons of the turf in golden days. But even they couldn't outdo the kid when he came to town.

CHAPTER 20
Superman

They are all here at Louisiana Downs. Everyone. Superman is here, Deadeye, Nacho Man, Jack The Ripper. Even The Rat is here. And Kody Kellenberger.

This is too good to be true. I first met Nacho Man just a week after arriving in the States. He was the outrider at Victory Haven training center in Lexington. He was friendly, smiling, and would often be found sat on his horse by the rail eating nachos. The last time I bumped into him was last September, in South Korea.

Keith 'Superman' Austin, an ex-jockey who nearly won the much coveted Missouri Derby back in the day, is here. I know him from his time as an exercise rider in Kentucky. He has worked for Tom Amoss, D Wayne Lukas and Mark Casse. He is wearing a different hat now, though. An owner gave him a shot. He has four horses, his trainer's license just issued, something the 46-year-old said he has always wanted to do. He should know his stuff with that background.

Another ex-rider training here is Guy Smith. Originally from Texas, he brought home well over 1,000 winners as a jockey. He has just a small string of horses, a trainer, a horseman, waiting for a good one.

Deadeye is here, partner of trainer Denise Schmidt. I met him at Fair Grounds over the winter. The Ripper has ridden some winners for their barn. Deadeye has had a colorful life. There are some people you don't ask about their nickname.

Jack 'The Ripper' Gilligan and his agent, Richie 'The Rat' Price, decided to stay south this summer instead of heading back to their usual Kentucky circuit after Fair Grounds. A lengthy lay-off due to injury in the New Year followed by the Covid shutdown, and the fact that a bunch of New York riders were heading to Kentucky while New York racing was yet to resume, made Churchill look too salty a prospect.

Richie the Rat hails from New Orleans. In his youth, he tried for a normal life. He spent time as a jewelry maker, but the lure of the track was too strong. It is like that for some people, not so much a job as a lifestyle. The Rat has been an agent for a long time now. He has Jack and Kody's book. They all share a house, and Richie is the designated cook.

Kody Kellenberger I didn't really know, but I had seen him exercising horses daily back at Keeneland. He rode well. I remember being at the gate one morning when the upstate New Yorker was jogging one toward the gate. It whipped around without notice, a sharp 180-degree about-turn. Not many riders sit that at a jog when they are riding short. He did – just. Sometimes just is enough.

He got his apprentice jockey license out, rode a winner on his first mount for Mike Maker. He went out to Arizona and rode at Turf Paradise, getting his fair share of winners. From there, he came to Fair Grounds, rode a few winners, then one came down with him. He broke his collarbone in the shadow of the winning post.

So, Gilligan and Kellenberger came here to get going again after injuries, and it's working out for both of them. Kellenberger has racked up ten winners already after a late start to the meet. Kody Kellenberger wasn't at Fair Grounds long enough for the locals to throw him a nickname as they did with Gilligan. Maybe 2K works

The Ripper wanted to get back in the winner's enclosure. A conversation with Karl Broberg had him hauling his tack to Louisiana Downs. The plan has been working out well. Broberg's string have been flying under the watchful eye of his assistant, Kevin Martin, who grew up here and wears a T-shirt well.

Gilligan has now ridden 32 winners, hitting at 24 percent, which leaves him five behind in the contest for leading rider. He is duking it out with Joel Dominguez, who rides for Steve Asmussen.

Louisiana Downs may be pretty small in reputation nowdays, but it is not small in size. The grandstand is pretty huge, square, and glass enclosed, to keep the sweltering summer heat at bay.

Attached to the grandstand is a casino with 800 slot machines, which, Covid or not, were doing pretty good business the Saturday I was there. Also on the racecourse grounds are three hotels and a restaurant. I stayed in one of the hotels and I was far from the only person there.

It was good to be back on a racecourse, I've been on a lot of them, in the UK, in Ireland, in France, in the USA, in Canada. I was even on a racecourse in South Korea once.

They come in all shapes and sizes, all flavors. The constant is the Thoroughbred horses, the jockeys in silks, and a winning post. And grizzled men trying to find that next winner.

Louisiana Downs was born in 1974. It was a popular venue boasting large crowds. Its feature race, the Super Derby, was a big hit. It obtained Grade 1 status. McCarron won it, Day won it, Stevens won it. Alysheba won it, Sunday Silence won it, Tiznow won it. They all won it. It boasted a million-dollar purse at its peak in the early 1990s. The purse last year was down to $300k, and the race is now reduced to Grade 3 status. This year the Covid crisis has caused its cancellation.

It makes for an exciting day for the smaller tracks, when a big chunk of money is put away for one big day of racing a year. Understandably some of the horsemen who have raced at the track all year don't always like it too much when they see a large amount of purse money they helped to generate head for the pockets of major outfits, who ship in for that one day and plunder. Even so, it puts the spotlight on the track nationally for that single day of the year, and Super Derby day used to fill that cavernous grandstand.

It's not Saratoga, but then Saratoga isn't Saratoga this year. It's a reminder though of how things were, before life in the time of Covid. People don't seem worried here, don't seem bothered. People are eating at the restaurants, sitting up at the bar drinking, things seemingly normal.

It was good to be at the races again, to see familiar faces again, to hear the thunder of hooves again. I missed the racetrack, talking about horses, watching horses race. Watching horses train. It's a primitive thing, but endlessly fascinating, and at its best one of the most dramatic spectacles man has contrived within the sporting arena. Zenyatta in the Classic, American Pharoah winning the Triple Crown, Affirmed and Alydar duelling in the Belmont Stakes, the stuff of legend.

Louisiana Downs is clean, friendly, neat, and the track is considered kind on horses. The commentator, John McGary, is enthusiastic, informed, and his energy keeps the show rolling along nicely through the day.

Most important though, of course, is simply that it's open. That's maybe all you really need to know.

I spent a summer at Saratoga a couple of years ago. I saw big dreams being realized there. Louisiana Downs is a purveyor of smaller dreams, but little fish taste sweet still.

Keith Austin was brought up 20 minutes from Louisiana Downs, so it was kind of nice that he had his first runner as a licensed trainer here, the homeboy in his hometown. It was even nicer that it won. Of course it won. It had to – he's Superman.

CHAPTER 21

Barclay Tagg & Tiz The Law

You might have been forgiven for thinking the 2003 Kentucky Derby victory of Funny Cide (like Tiz The Law a NY-bred owned by Sackatoga Stables) would have been highlight enough, that Tagg would have been content to drift into retirement after such an accomplishment. Not a bit of it. He and his partner and assistant trainer, Robin Smullen, just kept on going, and now, no less than 17 years later, they may be on the verge of an even greater highlight as the colt attempts to move closer to possible Triple Crown glory.

I've heard of late starters, but quite frankly I think Barclay Tagg is being ridiculous. He waited until he was 60 to meet his now partner, Robin Smullen. He was 65 before he decided he'd run one in the Kentucky Derby, and then he won it. And now, at 82, an age when your greatest ambition should probably be just to try to stay awake in your armchair long enough to watch the big race on TV, this man is going to hop in his car, drive the 12 hours from Saratoga to Louisville to saddle his horse, and he is going to try to win another Kentucky Derby nearly 20 years after his last one.

It's a far cry from the day it all started.

"I don't know how old I was – about 12, I suppose," he says. "We had stopped overnight in Saratoga to visit family on our way up for a vacation in Canada, like we did in the old days. I haven't taken much time off since! I was just walking around the town that evening and came across the Thoroughbred sale that was on, so I went in and saw everything that was going on, and I thought it was all fascinating."

After he returned home, young Tagg wanted to take pony-riding lessons, so he went to the local riding school with $10. That bought him three lessons. The proprietor told him to come along after school and help out and he would get all the riding he wanted.

"I ended up showing horses for some people, and then I went to college. By the time I got out of college (in 1961, with a degree in animal husbandry) I had a wife and a baby, so I got a job on a farm with a house."

Within a few years, though, he was learning to gallop Thoroughbreds. He learned well enough to end up becoming a professional steeplechase rider, at an age when a lot of steeplechase riders are deciding to hang up their boots. He had his share of winners but, by 1971, Tagg had decided he wanted to train horses.

"I was working for an Irishman, Charlie Kelly. He was just a great guy. I was breaking some yearlings for him. He got stuck with a horse – the owner didn't pay his bills – so he said to me to take it down to Maryland and see if we can win some money with it. So I did, and I got lucky. I didn't have a clue what I was doing."

Tagg did win money with it, and then Charlie Kelly found Tagg an owner who sent him two horses. One was an unraced 5-year-old. He won eight times with it, and Barclay Tagg had embarked on a 50-year career as a racehorse trainer. "If it hadn't been for Charlie, I don't know what would have happened, how I would have got started with no money or horses," he says.

He ticked along training three or four for well over a decade.By the mid-80s, though, business had picked up. The number of horses in his charge grew considerably – to nearly 100 at one point – and he won a lot of races.

Then in 1996, at the age of nearly 60, he met Robin Smullen, a horsewoman. She showed ponies as a girl, galloped Thoroughbreds as a teenager and trained racehorses as an adult. They teamed up, in life and on the track.

And then, just a few years later, along came **Funny Cide**. "Now he was a difficult horse, very difficult to ride," said Smullen. I asked if she galloped him. "Every day," she says. "He just wanted to try and go as fast as he could."

They won the Kentucky Derby with that horse, and the Preakness and the Jockey Club Gold Cup. What was then the trainer's best horse had came along at the age of 65. "It was something else," says Smullen.

For the best part of 20 years, the horseman and the horsewoman carried on training horses, training winners. They found some more good ones – Confrontation, Realm, Showing Up – and then, in 2018, Barclay Tagg was back at that Thoroughbred sale room in Saratoga, Robin beside him, and this time the hammer dropped in his direction for a $110,000 Constitution colt.

And he had another Derby horse.

I ask Smullen what the young Tiz The Law was like when he first trained. Some Constitutions aren't easy, talent and temperament quite often go hand in hand, and he had those hints of white around his eyes. Was he easy? "He is until he isn't," she says, laughing.

"The exercise riders were having trouble with him, so I got on him, and one day he reared up vertical three times, so high, in the shedrow. Now I can sit rearers, but I thought, 'holy crap, I don't know if I can stay on him.' After that, we kept him locked up. Juan [Barajas Saldana, stable foreman] leads him to the track and back, and Barclay ponies him and I ride him in his gallops and Heather [Smullen, her niece] breezes him."

Tagg says, "The first time I ponied him, he reared at me and hit me in the jaw with his knee. I thought he was going to take my head off. I couldn't eat for three days."

I suggest perhaps the horse has made amends for his early hooligan-like behavior. "He sure has," he says with a chuckle.

"We have a wonderful guy taking care of him, Juan Barajas Saldana, my foreman for over 20 years. He took him over, goes everywhere with him. So, between Robin, Heather and Juan, we have it pretty good. We keep a pretty tight hand on him."

Tiz The Law has a near-perfect race record, six wins from seven starts, the Champagne Stakes, the Holy Bull, the Florida Derby, the Belmont Stakes and most recently the Travers. He is a worthy favorite for the Kentucky Derby, the day after another race to savor in the Kentucky Oaks, in which another hot favorite, Gamine, goes head to head with the impressive Swiss Skydiver.

It's an undercard and a main event even Don King would be proud to pull off. They could be two races to shake off this year's seeming never-ending hangover. Let's hope so.

I think Barclay Tagg was lucky to meet Robin Smullen, and I think Tiz The Law was lucky to meet both of them.

It is likely that, in lesser hands, neither Funny Cide nor Tiz The Law would have had such outstanding race records. All those years, hands-on with horses, working it all out together. They say stayers win the race of life. I hope that is true.

I hope Tiz The Law stays healthy and lines up on the first Saturday in September. The date may be different but the contest is the same.

I shall cheer for Swiss Skydiver and Peter Callahan in the Kentucky Oaks, and I shall cheer for Tiz The Law in the Derby. I shall be cheering for Barclay, Robin, Heather and Juan. I think, though, my mind may be dwelling on a small boy, who long, long, ago stumbled upon a Thoroughbred auction at Saratoga one evening and the course of his life was changed forever.

CHAPTER 22

Cauthen, Stevens, McCarron: Three Greats

Three riders, over 70,000 races ridden between them, more than 13,000 winners, nearly $600 million in purses accumulated. Three Eclipse Award-winning Hall of Fame athletes with six Kentucky Derbies and 20 Breeders' Cup victories among a list of achievements too extensive to note here. Three legends of the sport who conducted their careers in the saddle to the highest standard and who have been longstanding global ambassadors for U.S. horse *racing.*

All three of these men support the Water Hay Oats Alliance. Patrick Lawrence Gilligan asked Chris McCarron, Steve Cauthen and Gary Stevens why.

McCarron: "I believe in a level playing field and that level playing field has to start at ground zero. That means no medication, let the horses run on their merits and see who is the best. I don't think it is in the long-term interest of the horses' health to be treating them with medications, to allow them to perform an exercise that they maybe would not be physically sound to do without them.

Cauthen: "I've never been a big fan of drugs in horses. As a jockey, not knowing what is in them, that's worrying. You don't want them running not even feeling their feet. But the bottom line is that it's not just that. The world nowadays doesn't want human athletes running on drugs and it doesn't want horses running on drugs either. We have to come in line with reality and hopefully give fans who bet on the sport more confidence that everyone is on a level playing field."

Stevens: "Everyday you go out there, you, as the rider, and the horse are at risk. It's a dangerous sport. But, when you have medications, even legal ones on raceday, I just do not believe that it's safe for equine or jockey, and this has long been my thought. We have 33 racing jurisdictions here [in the U.S.] with different sets of medication rules, and that's one reason I signed on."

The Horse Racing Integrity and Safety Act, has recently passed the House of Representatives, could you share your thoughts on the Act.

McCarron: "There are a lot of smart people who have been working on this for a long time, and I am with it because they have been working to have every state on board and one entity that could set medication guidelines.

"I would have the utmost faith in USADA (U.S. Anti-Doping Agency). They have been doing this for a long time. Some people may say, 'well, what the heck do they know about horse racing?' They don't need to know about horse racing, they just need to know about chemistry, what is legal and therapeutic and what is performance-enhancing.

"Because of USADA's experience in the field, I believe there is no better entity to organize this very daunting task. I have worked in supporting the passing of this act and have learnt a lot and I know in my heart I am on the right side of the fence."

Cauthen: "There needs to be one body that rules racing nationwide. The current model doesn't work. Everyone needs to be following the same rules everywhere. It needs to be run like any good business. I think the people are doing their jobs, but it is just different everywhere."

Stevens: "It's another step. I hope it comes about and it looks like it will, and absolutely it's the right direction and it will be a big day for horse racing."

The whip is another issue being debated with widely differing new rules being implemented or planned in several states. What are your views?

McCarron: "I like the idea of having to give the horse time to respond after it is struck before it can be used again because, obviously, if it doesn't move forward there's no point continuing hitting it.

"I was known as a rider that used the stick a lot, and I'm not proud of that at all, and if I was riding today I would definitely be working to change my style. A lot of fans don't want to see horses hit all the way down the stretch.

"I definitely don't think the whip should be taken away, or not being allowed to hit the horse at all, but I am in favor of limiting the number of strikes and not allowing horses to be struck multiple times in rapid succession."

Cauthen: "My view is that it needs to be dealt with within the industry and we need the same rules anywhere. A jockey needs a whip on a horse, they need it for their safety and the safety of their competitors, you have to be able to ride the horse, and the whip is part of what you ride the horse with.

"I think slapping down the shoulder and back-handers are not a problem. I'm not sure it's a numbers thing so much as just getting everyone together and coming up with one set of rules everywhere. I don't think good riders go bashing their horses and I don't think good trainers would want that anyway. But it doesn't make any sense whatsoever doing one thing in New Jersey, one thing in California, another thing in Kentucky."

Stevens: "I think limiting the number of strikes will make the good riders great and the average riders better, and some jockeys won't deal too well with it.

"Regarding the different rules everywhere, I would say to the guys, 'go out and test it for a couple of weeks then come and give some feedback.'

"I have no problem with the six-strike rule coming to California. What bothers me is a horse with absolutely no chance at the back of the field being flailed on. I have been doing raceday analysis for several years now, and I don't like to see that.

"But there is no way I would want to go out there to ride a race without being able to use the whip. Horses can get distracted out there. I was riding a horse called Storming Home, and it was well known you couldn't use the whip on him. He spotted a photographer in the infield, shied out and I ended up in an intensive care unit for five days."

How would you like to see the sport five years from now?

McCarron: "I'd like to see a contraction, maybe tracks limiting the length of some of their meets, and maybe even not having racing every day of the week. In the long term, I think the current trend toward contracting meets is heading in the right direction."

Cauthen: "I think it's a great sport and the more people get a chance to connect with it the better. When other sports were cancelled, viewing and betting on horseracing took off when television exposure increased on Fox Sports and the other channels. We have to keep reaching out, there is great racing and lots to look forward to, we just need to work on cleaning up our act and, when we have done that, there can be more time to focus on a great sport that produces great rivalries when horses meet. People love that."

Stevens: "I would like us to fall in line with international rules on medication with zero tolerance for raceday medication, and I would also like to see whip rules around the world unified, instead of each country having different rules.

"We have been the only show in town until recently, and our viewership on Fox Sports for our Saratoga live show has been unbelievably good. The indictments were horrible, but this bill can make it a good thing, because maybe without those arrests the bill may not have progressed."

CHAPTER 23

Robby Albarado & Swiss Skydiver

Albarado is a Spanish name, and Louisiana, where Robby Albarado was born, in Lafayette, was under the rule of the Kingdom of Spain from 1760 until 1802. Indeed the majority of the architecture found in the famous French Quarter of New Orleans is actually Spanish in style, the earlier French colonists' residences virtually eradicated by a series of major fires in the city.

Who knows if one of the jockey's ancestors arrived on these shores way back then, but the name Albarado (or Alvarado) is thought to have been one of the oldest Spanish surnames to be found in North American archives. Their coat of arms suggests they were successful seafarers, so perhaps it was fitting that Robby Albarado successfully raided Pimlico last Saturday like a pirate, and successfully made away with the bounty. He has been doing that for years now.

His father rode bush races as a young man, and young Robby stood and watched him in his earliest years.

Born in 1973, by the age of 12 he was following in his father's footsteps. By 16 young dark-eyed and sallow-skinned apprentice 'bug boy', Albarado was at Evangeline Downs, where he rode his first winner.

His career progressed smoothly at racetracks in Louisiana, Chicago and Arkansas. In his fifth year riding, he won his first Graded stakes. The first day he rode at Keeneland, in 1996, he rode a treble and then in 1998, at the age of 25, his tack at Churchill Downs, he won his first Grade 1.

It wasn't all milk and honey though. He fractured his skull in 1998, and again in 1999, a titanium mesh still in his skull now. In 2000, he suffered head trauma again.

From 2000 until 2010, Robby Albarado hovered just in or out of the top ten riders nationally. In 2004, he won the George Woolf Memorial Jockey Award. That same year he notched his 3,000th career victory.

In 2007 and 2008, he rode the champion Curlin. They won a host of top stakes races, including the Breeders' Cup Classic and the Dubai World Cup. He was invincible. The gods were smiling on him – or so it seemed.

In 2011, Albarado was to ride Animal Kingdom in the Kentucky Derby. Three days before the big day, a horse threw him and kicked him before a race, breaking his nose. Connections of the horse were concerned Albarado wasn't in a condition to take the mount and replaced him.

He proved fit enough to win a couple of stakes that first weekend in May at Churchill Downs, Albarado, but he was on the sidelines when Animal Kingdom won the Derby.

With hindsight, that lost mount may have been important. From 2012 onwards, the rider whose mounts regularly banked around $10 million a year now won only half that.

And then, in 2019, business really dipped. The jockey with over 5,000 career wins and three Breeders' Cup victories to his name managed just 24 wins, albeit with time off due to injuries. And then, this year, the wheels really came off.

Prior to Saturday, October 3, Robby Albarado had managed 21 wins. A man who in his best season bagged close to $20 million in 12 months had managed less than $400,000 in nine.

Swiss Skydiver carried all before her this year, crowned by an impressive victory in the G1 Alabama Stakes at Saratoga before a second in the Kentucky Oaks, both times ridden by Tyler Gaffalione.

Robby Albarado didn't have a ride anywhere on Preakness day, and on the days he did it was generally at Indiana Downs now, and even there his services were not much in demand.

And then he got a phone call. The gods remembered him.

Gaffalione had unexpectedly defected. Mike Smith had ridden the filly previously, but his agent didn't commit either. They decided they wouldn't travel to Pimlico to ride the filly in the Preakness, where she was due to take on the colts, including the winner of the Kentucky Derby.

It was such a bold call by the trainer it left some shaking their heads. And then the trainer made an even bolder one. He called the rider, who was colder than Alaska, and he was booked to ride Swiss Skydiver in the 145th running of the Preakness Stakes.

A filly in the Preakness? In 144 runnings, only five had ever emerged victorious, and this filly had been beaten in her previous race, one restricted to her own sex.

She probably shouldn't have been there, and what was Albarado doing on her back? His last winner before he rode the Preakness was 13 days previously at Indiana Downs in $10,000 maiden claimer for Indiana-breds. That was his confidence builder for taking on Authentic.

He had two rides at the Pimlico meet before being legged up on Swiss Skydiver. They both finished last. In the 12 days leading up to Preakness day, he had taken part in just nine races.

Yet he produced a masterclass in race-riding. This from a rider so washed up he should have been covered in seaweed.

The boldness of the entry was matched by the boldness of the jockey. Robby Albarado is a decisive rider, he comes out of the gates and puts his horse where he has already decided it will be, and the horse doesn't look like it gets much say in the matter.

Five furlongs out, Albarado was sat on the rail, just behind Authentic. By the four pole, he had moved off the rail and slipped past Authentic and stolen the lead, and maybe just as importantly the Pimlico rail entering the home turn. It was a breathtaking, confident, race-winning maneuver, a tactical display from a virtuoso. But still it wasn't over.

Down the stretch, the Kentucky Derby winner bore down on her, gunning for her, matching her. But Albarado and Swiss Skydiver locked together. They looked Velazquez and Authentic in the eyes, and they won the Preakness Stakes by a neck.

There was no crowd there to cheer. But all around the nation, where people gathered around a television screen, fans erupted. It was a duel, a race to match Affirmed and Alydar in the Belmont Stakes. A race that will live in people's memories, a race that makes people remember why they love this sport so much.

So Albarado is back. In the most unmistakable way possible, he demonstrated why he has been one of the nation's top riders for so many years.

People had forgotten him. They won't forget him again. He will be back in demand again, riding the big races again, his tack at Keeneland and Churchill again, where it always belonged.

I hope he will be sat in his corner again, chatting with Todd, his valet, again, in turn criticizing or praising and helping my son Jack, who sits next to him in those jockeys' rooms again, as he always did, since the young lad first entered the Churchill Downs room and Todd Taylor took him under his wing.

Russian artist Valeriy Gridnev drew a portrait of Robby and Jack standing in the paddock at Keeneland one year. There were three of them, Robby holding court. The old master and the sophomore stood opposite one another. It came up for auction at Keeneland and Jack bought it. I think it may have gone up in value now.

That is the tale of Robby Albarado, a tale of outrageous fortune and misfortune and a comeback so spectacularly dramatic and unlikely that, although it would make a great movie, who on earth would ever believe it?

CHAPTER 24

Ed Prosser

Although racefans get to know the horses, the riders and the trainers involved in the sport, there are many involved in the industry who, within it, are as widely known to insiders as the likes of Bob Baffert and Frankie Dettori are to the general betting public. Ed Prosser is one of those people.

Whether you are with racing people in a pub in Dublin, a nightclub in Moscow, a Chinese restaurant in Newmarket or a hotel in Kazakhstan, if you are truly among racing people and you ask them, "Do you know Ed Prosser?" the response will be in the affirmative. And it will be given with a smile. Everyone knows Ed Prosser. And everyone likes him.

Prosser is two parts Hugh Grant to one part Johnny English, finished off with thick-lensed spectacles and grey hair, and he speaks like old money, a proud Yorkshireman, born to a family fond of horses and horse racing. Educated at the prestigious Oundle School in Northamptonshire, he took a degree in history at Royal Holloway in London. In his case, though, both seats of learning seemed to become more a base for ventures to the races than institutions of deep scholarship.

After university, Prosser got a place on the British Horseracing Board's graduate course. That gave him a taste of work experience in the industry. He had spells with the Levy Board, the horseracing forensics lab, and a couple of racecourses.

A year later, he got a position with news and PR agency *Racenews*, which involved him spending long days and evenings at Tattersalls auctioneers in Newmarket, typing out sales reports for the *Sporting Life* and then the *Racing Post*, and it was then, through a mutual friend, that I got to know him. He ended up owning shares in various horses I trained over the years. He says he has had shares in horses with a lot of very good trainers, and Pat Gilligan.

We had fun, landed some gambles, drank some beer. And then, eight years ago, Prosser got a job with Keeneland – the highest-grossing Thoroughbred sales company in the world – as its European representative.

Prosser is perfect for the job. Although he could not be more the typical old-fashioned public-school-educated English gentleman, he is one of only a few Anglo-Saxons who can carouse easily in a crowded bar with the Murphia, or who can be found comfortably downing vodkas in Dudleys in downtown Lexington with Russian clientele, or, on occasion, even fermented horse milk in Kazakhstan, or even chewing on goat's tongue in the Saudi desert.

"I only cover a small part of the world really, but Keeneland sells horses throughout South America, Central America, the Caribbean, Europe, Russia, Kazakhstan, the Middle East, South Africa, Australia,

Japan, South Korea and many other places. Perhaps our biggest international customer base, though, in terms of number of variety of clients for foals, yearlings and mares is Ireland.

"We bill the September Sale as the world's yearling sale, and there really is no other auction of its kind globally, offering the best of dirt and turf horses at the same time."

He adds, "This year Keeneland graduates won the 2000 Guineas [Kameko], one of only a few 2020 European Classic winners to have been offered at public auction, the winners of both the Kentucky Derby [Authentic] and Oaks [Shedaresthedevil] changed hands with us, the Swedish Derby winner [BullofWall Street] was bought here, the UAE Oaks winner [Down On Da Bayou], Grade 1 winners in Australia and Japan, and the winner of a $1.5 million race in Saudi Arabia. We have even had a Classic winner in recent years in Kazakhstan, where racing is centered around Almaty in the south of the country."

Prosser has been to Turkey, which he says is run very efficiently by the Turkish Jockey Club, and its stallion ranks were bolstered considerably last year by the purchases of Daredevil, Super Saver, Trappe Shot and Bodemeister. He has also travelled of course all around Europe and the Middle East. Where Keeneland does business east of New York, Prosser has probably been there.

There are five principal racetracks in Russia where they race mainly on dirt. The Central Moscow Hippodrome, which boasts a grand exterior, has held race meets since 1834. This year's Russian Derby was won by a son of Constitution sold at Keeneland for $40,000 by Pope McLean and family, of Crestwood Farm in Kentucky.

Prosser has a contact list any bloodstock agent would pay a million dollars for. He plays his cards close to his chest, but lets juicy tidbits out at times. His role is varied, he might arrange the purchase of a session-topper for a sheikh, or lunch for an ex-trainer down on his luck. He travels extensively (in normal times), promoting Keeneland sales, and promotes also its spring and autumn race meets, annual highlights of the Lexington social calendar (in normal times).

Wherever Keeneland customers are to be found, whether in Sweden, or Bahrain, or home in the UK, then Prosser is there to support and assist them. Whatever he does, whatever the task, he seems to quietly and efficiently execute it, while at the same time wearing an air of slight surprise at his situation.

Kentucky trainer Phil Sims was apparently so impressed by Ed Prosser after getting to know him that he named a horse after him – seemingly overlooking the opportunity to immortalize the fruits of his own loins. There was to be no Matt's Kitten, no Blake's Kitten, there is however now a Prosser's Kitten. It can hopefully be of some small solace to his presumably disgruntled sons that at least the filly proved less than distinguished on the racecourse and now plies her trade in New Mexico.

Most jobs in racing are not front-of-house, not played in the public eye, but many of them afford the opportunity to meet people from all walks of life and different places, and sometimes to travel to exotic destinations they didn't think they'd ever visit.

It draws the world together quite well, horseracing. As does Ed Prosser.

CHAPTER 25

Chel-C Bailey

Cross training refers to taking up activities or sports away from an athlete's primary arena in order to improve total fitness and strength by working on muscle groups that the athlete's primary sport maybe does not maximally exercise.

Golfer Bryson DeChambeau is an example of cross training improving a professional athlete's game. During the Covid lockdown, he bulked up and strengthened up. He put on 40lbs of muscle, working out in the gym daily, and improved his drive by over 20 yards consistently. His game improved to such an extent that he won the U.S. Open in September and is now world #6.

There are proponents who say playing sports other than your primary one can actually enhance performance. In the UK, jockey Francis Norton had experienced considerable success in both boxing and horseracing at an early age until, eventually, he had to decide which path to pursue. He chose horseracing and, at the age of 49, is still a top rider.

Chel-c Bailey was a state champion high-school wrestler, competing against boys in middle school and throughout high school. She went on to become a professional Mixed Martial Arts (MMA) fighter. She has now chosen horseracing as her vocation and the apprentice rider landed a benchmark debut victory at Keeneland recently on her first ride at the track.

Bailey's first experience of riding was hopping on other people's horses bareback in her native Washington State, which is where she calls home. She also did some grooming for an Arabian racehorse outfit, which gave her considerable insight.

Horses, though her first passion, were, for a long time, left on the back burner due to her wrestling and MMA commitments.

"My professional record is three wins, no losses," she says. "I wanted to try and become a UFC fighter, but they don't have my weight class, which is atomweight (105lb). I was fighting women at strawweight (115lb), so I was fighting opponents much bigger than me."

Horses were a childhood obsession for Bailey. "I'd watch horseracing movies, read books and say 'I want to be a jockey'. Horses have always been my favorite animals, and I have always loved being around them, but wrestling and fighting took over and I went away for college to Oklahoma City university, which had the best women's wrestling team in the United States.

"None of my family or friends had any connection to horseracing, and I didn't know anyone, or even how to get into it, until I met my husband, David (an exercise rider), in Las Vegas while living there for fighting. Our first conversation was about Husqvarna chainsaws and Thoroughbred racehorses.

"David started working for Chris Hartman at Oaklawn in Arkansas, and I began out at a farm there for Hillary Hartman and started learning from the ground up."

Bailey says she had a pony as a kid, but she never wanted to put a saddle on it. "It took too long, so I would just throw my leg over it and ride it bareback," she says.

"I have a low centre of gravity from wrestling and I did a lot of snowboarding, skiing and skateboarding when I was younger, which I think helped with balance when David began teaching me to gallop.

"And then, after my very first race, it felt like I was back to day one, having my first gallop. It's a whole different ball game. Even breezing a horse versus riding in a race is a completely different thing. You're not just sitting rating one, there are many more components to it. It's multi-tasking, It's 180 degrees difference.

She believes that, pound-for-pound, jockeys are stronger than fighter.

"In fighting you are pushing and pulling and punching and kicking, using every muscle in your body in different ways but for different purposes. I would say jockeys have more balance and more finesse and their type of strength is different. I think jockeys have more agility, have different upper body, shoulder, thigh and core strength and have different split-second cognitive decisions to make.

"And, of course, they need to be able to ride and control a Thoroughbred racehorse at top speed, and they also need to be able to maintain their weight under 120lbs

"I find quite a few correlations with fighting in relation to race-riding. Driving and pushing out a horse, there is some similarity, using your shoulders, both hands punching forward and using your back muscles, using your thighs, using your core."

There is another major difference between the two disciplines. "The thing I find difficult is that, when I'm fighting, I have a coach, a mentor who teaches you and helps you," she says. "You don't have that being a jockey.

"I know I have a lot to work on, to improve and polish up on, but I know I have a lot of ability, heart desire and determination. I have been trying to figure it out myself and that is quite difficult.

"When you are out there, you are out there to race. It is cool and neat to have fans cheering at the races. It's awesome to have that support but, when you're coming down the lane and in the final drive, you're focused on winning the race and everything that's going on in the race, the same as fighting.

"My 12-month apprentice [bug] year doesn't begin until after my next win and, with all the restrictions with Covid making traveling to different tracks difficult, I am in no rush for that to start yet, so I am enjoying mostly galloping for Michelle Lovell for now.

"I'm apple-picking a bit at the moment. I really want to ride, but I feel that waiting might be the best option right now."

Bailey is not going to race-ride now until the spring, when she intends to compete in the mid-Atlantic around Maryland. It's an intelligent move, apprentices only get a year to claim after their fifth win, there is plenty of racing in that circuit and you don't have the top jocks you get in Kentucky.

Since her first winner at Oaklawn Park in February, Chel-c Bailey has now won four from 82 as a rider, including a win on October 8 at Keeneland by a nose and a neck, getting up in the last stride under a cool come-from-the-back ride. It was a victory all the more laudable as her stick was knocked out of her hand during the race

I told her that happens to the best. It happened to nine-time Epsom Derby winner Lester Piggott in France many years ago. He didn't let it phase him, he just moved alongside another rider, got in rhythm with him, and snatched the stick out of the surprised jockey's hand. He rode the horse out for second, and the other, now whipless rider, finished a close third.

When the crowd realized what had happened, there was uproar and the bewildered stewards immediately called an enquiry. They called Piggott in, and Piggott gave them the highly unlikely story that the other rider, when he realized Piggott was without a stick, offered the great man his own whip out of the kindness of his heart.

"But what did you say to him," asked the incredulous stewards.

"I said le baton, si vous plait." claimed Piggott.

The horse was demoted, Piggott was banned, and the French crowd lapped up the replay, cheering with delight at the outrageous tactics deployed against one of their own. By that evening, the story was all over the news on both French and English television.

Now I am not suggesting for one moment that Chel-c Bailey, 10lb apprentice rider, should ever consider such a ploy if she ever found herself in such a predicament again, but I am pretty sure she would have the nerve for it.

CHAPTER 26

Pajeen Delp

I only ever spoke to Pajeen Delp once, when she and my son Jack shared an apartment in Louisville during a meet at Churchill Downs.

She was young and pretty and gentle and ladylike, and she had a big bright smile and soft eyes.

She passed away recently, suddenly, at the age of just 37. She suffered from low blood pressure. She just fell asleep and never woke up. Natural causes. She stayed sleeping gently as those who loved her wept.

Mimi Davis, my friend and sometime work colleague knew Pajeen for the best part of nine years, from when Pajeen stayed with her during a spring meet at Keeneland. Mimi asked if I could say something for her.

She told me about Pajeen's passing, how she was friends with Pajeen and her mother, Regina. She told me how clever Pajeen was. Her grades meant she could have studied at either veterinary or medical school.

Pajeen was the daughter of Hall-of-Fame trainer Buddy Delp, the man who trained 1979 Kentucky Derby winner Spectacular Bid, a four-time champion. Delp said he was the greatest horse ever to look through a bridle.

Mostly, though, Mimi just told me how nice she was, how sometimes she seemed overlooked, as quiet, nice people sometimes are. And she told me how kind she was, and knowledgeable about horses. In fact, if Mimi ever needed to know about a certain medication or drug she had never heard of, she would quickly text Pajeen for advice.

Mimi told me how close Pajeen was to her mother, how they spoke virtually every day, how Mimi spent Thanksgiving with them in New Orleans.

Later I spoke with Regina. "I feel like my sense of gravity Is all askew," she said. "My mind is not able to concentrate. The silence from her is very painful. We would talk and laugh together every day. She was my best friend and she told me I was hers. It's been very hard.

"My sister didn't have children, so Pajeen was like her baby too. We are going to meet up with Pajeen's friends in May. Mimi said we would all get together. She was loved by a lot of people. Aside from her own family, she had a family of friends at the racetrack as well.

"She was born in New Orleans. I never thought I would have children. I was 34. We named her *Pegeen*, which means 'little pearl' in the Gaelic language, but someone in *Racing Form* printed her name after her birth as *Pajeen*. So we decided to keep it!

"When Pajeen was about 12, the *Racing Form* ran a short story competition for people with interesting tales to tell. She wrote in and told them how she got her name and she won the competition. They sent her a *Racing Form* mug!"

Regina said Pajeen had an enquiring mind. "She was a real renaissance woman. I took her to plays and museums and zoos as a child in New Orleans and Chicago.

"When she was a little girl, I told her she had been so good that I would like to get her something she didn't have that she would really like. I did that twice for her. The first time she asked for a telescope, the second time she asked for a Latin/English dictionary so she could learn the roots of English words. I said, okay …

"She took her SAT's and they were so high, she skipped 12th grade and went straight to college. She spoke French and Spanish fluently.

"When she went to the University of Maryland, she was taking grade 3 courses that seniors would take."

Pajeen and her year-younger brother, Cleve, had been walking hots by the age of ten at their father's barn and moved on to ponying and then galloping. So, Pajeen decided to eschew veterinary or medical school to work at the track as assistant to several trainers. She even trained together with her brother in their own right for a period.

"But her last two times as assistant, she was humiliated by the trainers and treated very badly. I could tell she was depressed, so I went to see her in New Orleans. I have a bitterness towards them because of that. She didn't deserve that. She was very knowledgeable about horses."

In 2017, Pajeen decided to walk away from the racetrack. She worked in a library for a while, and applied to go study to become a nurse.

Early this year, she returned to the track to save money in case she was accepted for school. She took an assistant position with Richard Baltas in California, her first time out there. That was where she passed away two months ago. Regina said how helpful and kind Baltas and his wife had been. How they had helped her so much.

"I was so pleased to see some of the comments on *Facebook* from her friends in racing, and I was touched with what so many people said," Regina said. "It made me feel better to know that they will sincerely miss her because that means she conducted her life with dignity and love. It really helped me.

"Her acceptance letter for nursing school arrived last week."

I've known something like this before. The same thing really. Another good young person, he would ride a couple of sets for me. He had served his country in the UK and now wanted to work in racing. He tried to get a license to ride as an amateur over jumps. I promised to give him some rides, but the authorities kept turning him down.

He just didn't wake up one day. He had experienced a fit before apparently, which was why he couldn't be licensed to ride races. He didn't want to be champion rider or anything, just to pull the silks on a couple of times, experience the rush of the race. Life couldn't even give him that.

They say the good sometimes die young. Why wouldn't God want them up there with him, rather than down here among the pain and struggle.

I was brought up Catholic but do not practice now. I hope, though, I have some spirituality, and even though the odds of me making it to the good place are about 200/1 and drifting, If I do ever make it there, then I will have some tough questions to ask.

It is a fact, though, that every eternal atom we are created from, all the trillions and trillions of them, shall one day be a part of something else. Maybe the breeze running through your hair, or a rain drop running down your cheek, Regina. Maybe part of a big kind smile, or shining brown eyes. Perhaps a part of a blade of grass or a pretty flower, or a foal running in a field. Or a mighty oak.

I think that is why at times I have taken some comfort in the words of the poet: Mary Elizabeth Frye.

Do not stand at my grave and weep,
I am not there I do not sleep,
I am in a thousand winds that blow,
I am the softly falling snow,
I am the gentle showers of rain,
I am the fields of ripening grain,
I am in the morning hush,
I am in the graceful rush
Of the beautiful birds in circling flight,
I am the star shine of the night,
I am in the flowers that bloom,
I am in a quiet room.
I am in the birds that sing,
Do not stand at my grave and cry,
I am not there I did not die.

Pajeen was 'the light of our lives', her mother told me. What can I add to that.

In memory.

CHAPTER 27

Asmussen & Sons

When I was younger, working in the racing industry in Europe, the name Asmussen meant only one thing: Cash.

He was a superstar there for two decades, every bit as successful in France at that time as his compatriot Steve Cauthen was in Britain. Five times Cash was France's champion jockey. He was an Arc winner, he won four French Derbys and every French Classic at least once, and more than 70 G1s worldwide. If there had been a TRC Global Rankings back then, he would have been a regular in the higher reaches of the world top ten.

After I arrived in the States in 2014, Cash Asmussen had disappeared from the public eye. I knew he had retired from race-riding in 2001 and had immediately departed France and returned to the States, so I wondered what he had been up to since then, and how now it was his younger brother, Steve, who was the family flag bearer.

I met up with Steve Asmussen at Fasig Tipton in Lexington recently to ask about their careers and to piece together the family dynamic. And that, naturally, led back to their dad …

Keith Asmussen Sr

"I was born into the horse business," says Keith Asmussen Sr. "My dad, and my grandad were in the business. My dad trained five or six at a time, rode a little bit, raised horses. We were living in South Dakota, but my father ran them all over, from New England to Tijuana.

"I was riding match races by the age of 12. I rode Thoroughbreds first but got a bit heavy, so I rode Quarter Horse races for about 38 years."

Asmussen Sr was leading rider in Albuquerque in New Mexico, South Texas and other places, and he made a pretty good living. "I had a bad knee most of the time. I got cow-kicked by a horse when I was about ten, and I have had to put up with that damn thing most of my life.

"I was breaking a lot of babies, but that's a tough job seven or eight months of the year in South Dakota.

"I was riding first call for Wayne Lukas back then. I was riding for him before he was D. Wayne Lukas," he says with a chuckle."

Lukas sent him to South Texas to ride a futurity race one February. "It was 86 degrees, and it was about minus 2 degrees when I got back to South Dakota, so I asked my wife 'are you ready to move one more time?'"

That was in 1967. Marilyn, his wife of 59 years, whom he has known since he was about five – two kids who both loved horses – said yes. "She's about got me trained. She's been working on it," he says. "That's how I ended up in Laredo [in Texas], for the weather."

"I always knew how to work," he says. "I broke horses, rode races, hauled trailers, shod horses."

I ask him what he did in his spare time. He laughs, and without missing a beat says, "I rode more horses."

"In 1979, we set up El Primero training center [in Laredo] with Cash. We have 400 stalls here now and 95 percent of the horses we start here will end up going to Steve. We have a bunch of Tapits [Tapit] was broken in by Keith for the Winchell family, a family that has sent him horses for the past 41 years], Into Mischiefs, Uncle Mos, all of them. Cash is on one side of the track and I train on the other."

It was around then that another branch of the family business began. "My dad was wearing my mom out dragging her around the country," says Keith Asmussen. "So I set up a tack store [Asmussen Horse & Rider Equipment], which she ran for about 30 years. It's still going."

But back to his sons. "I'm real proud of those two boys, how they took off," he says. "They grew up on the farm. Steve had a groom's license when he was 12. There is a picture of him on the front of a magazine after we won a big race in New Mexico. Cash galloped his first Thoroughbred when he was nine.

"They were both good workers, although Steve liked to sneak off to the track kitchen sometimes. We have six grandchildren, and they all like to help on the farm too when they are home from university."

I say how positive Steve and Cash seemed when I spoke to them. I asked if that came from his parents. "Well, we're part of the same family you know," he says with a laugh. I walked into that one.

Cash Asmussen

"We were fortunate to follow in the footsteps of our parents, great mentors, who gave us an opportunity to practice what was to be our profession, working side by side away from the racetrack," he says. "We couldn't have made up for that time later on. We were learning from when we could walk. I believe we owe a lot of our success to that. We are still learning every day and our greatest teacher is the horse.

"The luxury of a jockey, to be associated with horses, with great horses, is to manage the energy of your partners, and the best way to do that is by communicating with them, and the better your horsemanship, the better you communicate.

"I feel in any equine sport, when the horse and rider become one, it is poetry in motion.

"I was prepared by my father and mother, but I couldn't have fathomed what was ahead of me."

Cash Asmussen, born Brian Keith Asmussen (he changed his name to Cash in 1977), won on his first ride, in 1978, for his mother, at Sunland Park racetrack in New Mexico, and even now he says that was one of the three greatest wins of his life.

The second was winning a Grade 3 at Aqueduct on Valid Expectations in November 1996 for his brother.

Cash went on to ride over 900 winners in just over three years riding Stateside, picking up an Eclipse Award for leading apprentice in 1979.

"I moved to New York toward the end of 1978. McCarron was in the room, Cordero, Velasquez, Pincay, Vasquez. It was a great education, and you needed to bring you're A game. If you didn't, don't bother showing up. Those guys could do things on a horse that most people couldn't do on foot."

It was the great Argentinian trainer Angel Penna who recommended Cash Asmussen to legendary French trainer Francois Boutin, who was looking for a rider for his owner Greek shipping billionaire Stavros Niarchos. Boutin acceded.

Asmussen says, "Penna told me in no uncertain terms that, if I wanted to see a beautiful part of the world from the backs of beautiful horses, I needed to think seriously about this opportunity. And how right he was.

"I was dropped into France on my head, but landed on my feet. And I came well armed – with Boutin and Niarchos behind me.

"It was still tough, though. I wasn't that well received at first, so believe me it was no hardship to not be able to understand or read French! It was good for my weight, though, struggling to order food. But I think I gained their respect in the end, and I say that with pride. I learnt to speak fluent French also in the end – because I was getting hungry

He recalls one time he was in a car with Boutin. "I was returning home after racing with Francois. He was driving and smoking his Davidoff No.2. We were having a bit of a disagreement about one of the rides I gave his horse, and I was trying to explain it when he took his cigar out of his mouth, turned to me and said, 'Cash, I think I preferred it when you couldn't speak French'.

"But the backing and support of Francois Boutin and Mr Niarchos gave me confidence. I hope I left something for racing. I will never have given it as much as it gave me."

It looked such a glamorous life, glamorous times, back then, Cash cutting a dash. Did it feel like that?

"It would be disrespectful to not say we led a glamorous life. Icons are hard or impossible to replace. Who replaces Francois Boutin? Who replaces Yves St Martin? Who replaces Henry Cecil? Who replaces Lester Piggott? Those were glamorous times and they made the game glamorous and, in turn, the game made them glamorous. Those superstars are hard, if not impossible, to replace."

By the end of his time in Europe, Cash was well loved in France. He had won five riders' titles, the only non-French jockey ever to have won one back then. “Allez Cash!” was the call at the Paris tracks for 20 years.

And of the places? “If Deauville was racing eight months a year, I might still be riding!”

But Cash Asmussen rode all over the world. G1 victories in seven countries on three continents – Japan, Hong Kong, Ireland, England, France, Canada and the USA.

“It was an education and a luxury you couldn’t pay for, to ride some of the greatest horses on some of the most beautiful racetracks in the world. Great horses take humans where we can’t go alone.”

I mention that the Middle East is missing from his resume. He says ‘yes’, laughing, “but my brother saw there was a bit of prize money to be picked up there so he went over and won the Dubai World Cup with Curlin!”

His brother had his back. Maybe he has to get over for the Melbourne Cup next? “I’ve been over for what I call the old timers’ race there. They call it the champions’ race. Melbourne was beautiful and great people.”

So many horses, but he says Suave Dancer has to come top of his list of greats.

“My dad bought him at Keeneland and he was broken at Laredo. I got to know him that winter, then he was sent to John Hammond in France for his owner, Monsieur Chalhoub, where I was reunited with him.”

Cash’s parents were there, in Paris, at Longchamp racecourse, when Cash Asmussen and Suave Dancer won the 1991 Prix de l’Arc de Triomphe.

Those were heady days, and, at El Primero training center, he is planning more with the help of his partner, Erica.

"She rides them, buys the shampoo, does just about everything, and puts up with me as well." he says. He also has his three daughters' assistance when they are home from university.

"We've got horses here, a full brother to a Derby winner, Uncle Mos, Tapits, Gun Runners – and they are a great-looking bunch too. I couldn't wait to get on them. If some people didn't like Steve Asmussen last year, they're going to hate him next year!

"I think what keeps me fresh is that, if a horse is capable of doing something and he's not doing it for me, because I'm not explaining it properly, then I've got to look at the man in the mirror.

"I'm a good guy. I just want to kick ass, show what I can do, and complement the horse!"

Steve Asmussen

Steve Asmussen has just trained his 9,000th winner. His son, Keith, was race riding for him during the summer.

"It was beyond describable to go through the process with him. He ended up winning a $100k stakes on a horse part-owned by my parents and a long-time client, and to see him succeed and feel good about himself was such a reward from a sport that has given us so much.

"My father is just an animal lover of the umpteenth degree. To come from a true Ma-and-Pa operation to where we are now, what it means to me, what we have achieved, is hard to describe.

"It was like watching my son ride and wanting him so hard to succeed. I had wanted to be a jockey, but I grew to six feet, and my son is similarly vertically challenged at five ten."

Steve, who has been a TRC world top-ten trainer for much of the year, did follow in his elder brother's footsteps and became a jockey for a while, but he was too tall and weight defeated him. Perhaps that track kitchen had been his undoing.

Talking about his riding career, though, Steve says, "The thing about Cash is he never understood why everyone couldn't do what he could."

"Now to stand here at 55, I am just at the center of a perfect storm. I love the input from all my family, their help, everyone is involved. And the long-time assistants I have are well known.

"The success we have achieved thanks to the horses, the feelings they have given us, makes us want more. I am still more surprised at our defeats than our successes. There are still huge things left to do. In fact, the urgency feels more now than ever before."

I mention how unlikely it was for two brothers to achieve two Eclipse awards in different spheres in the sport. "We keep very good company if nothing else," he smiles. "Maybe there's something in the water down there in Laredo!

"One of the great pleasures of my life is people who know my parents, and my parents' example, how they go about doing their best every day, not some days – every day. It's not a situation of measuring where you are at, you just work on getting better. In fact, it is alarming sometimes when you look back and realize how ignorant you were previously.

"All the family is heavily involved in our business. I love their input. My boys are much smarter than me. Growing up in a racing family, nothing you are doing is alone. My wife, Julie, the boys, Keith, Darren, and Eric, my parents, my brother, his family all involved. There might be just one name wrote down, but it is everyone and I love that. Horseracing is the vocabulary of the Asmussen family."

Finally I ask him, when he set out, did he ever think he would scale these heights? Soon to be the winning-most racehorse trainer ever in North America. "Frankly," he says, "I can't believe it took me so long to get here!"

So, when the Asmussens sit down at the dinner table to celebrate the holiday, we know the talk shall be of horses. There will be Cash with his Cashisms, the boys Keith, Darren and Eric chipping in, Cash's girls, Catherine, Carolyn and Christine, too. Grandad will be cracking jokes, the wives, mothers, partners, all a part of it. And Steve Asmussen sat right in the middle of his perfect storm.

But make no mistake, although Cash and Steve Asmussen are the spectacular fireworks, Keith Asmussen Sr has been the constant flame, the father, the husband, the horseman.

The man who broke in Tapit and Suave Dancer, and thousands more, the man who rode races for 38 years, even with that damn knee! He loves his family and his horses. And I loved talking with him.

CHAPTER 28

The One That Got Away

I missed Shanghai Moon a while back. Had him under my care in the spring when I worked as an assistant to Kentucky trainer Kenny McPeek. An attractive neat grey colt by Shanghai Bobby. He went pretty nicely in his early breezes. Maybe not at the top of our pecking order, but definitely signs of ability. I put him in my mental notebook – watch him first time, bet him second time out.

I watched him run first time. He got stuffed. Beaten over twenty lengths in a Maiden at Ellis Park Racecourse in Western Kentucky. I couldn't back him second time out on that performance. Second time out he ran even worse, finished last. I was puzzled. He should be better than that.

On his third start Kenny dropped him to maiden claiming, but for a tag of $150,000 at Churchill Downs. Not much of a drop, I thought. He added blinkers also. They would need to work a miracle.

They did. He won by three-quarters of a length under Julien Leparoux – at 33/1.

We have all been there, everyone who bets. The one that got away, the bet they were going to make but didn't. The one they let slip through their fingers.

You might think missing a 33/1 shot might sting a bit. Not really. I've missed bigger. I've missed much bigger. You couldn't believe the payday I missed out on, from a bet I didn't make. Go on, have a go. What's your biggest miss? What did it cost you? The ante-post 100/1 shot you were going to bet? The pick 4? The pick 6 even? Go on, knock yourself out, I will laugh at you. It will be a drop in the ocean compared to what I missed.

What's that? You play the lottery every week, same numbers. And the one week you didn't buy a ticket…Cost you what? Twenty million you say? That's a joke! Nothing! Pick yourself up man! Stop feeling sorry for yourself! I'm going to make you feel better! That's small change compared to the bet I didn't make! What's that? I'm full of what you say? I'm afraid not my friend. What I am going to tell you is true. I wish it wasn't.

I'm going back to around 2010. I was training horses in Newmarket in the UK, just a handful of cheap runners, getting by, nothing much happening, the odd gamble landed and Champagne for a while.

I used to subscribe to New Scientist. Don't ask me why really. I like to read and have an enquiring mind. And I suppose I wondered if I might stumble across something that I might make a mental lateral jump with to do with my day job, might have a light bulb moment, maybe.

So, one day I read an article in the magazine about this new thing that, as I understood it, was going to be a kind of online cash. Digital money. Everything was about the internet back then. The new frontier. It made sense to me. And what I really liked was that, the way the logarithm was written that produced (mined, they called it) the cash, there could only ever be a finite amount of it.

Twenty-one million bitcoins – that was the most there could ever be. That's not much, I thought. What if it took off? What if everyone wanted to buy and sell stuff online using these bitcoins, as they were called? There weren't enough of them. That would swell the value of each coin beyond imagination possibly.

I messed about on a piece of paper and thought over $100,000 a coin would be possible if it took off as the internet currency.

I decided to buy three hundred pounds worth. They were worth nothing, a few pennies each. I had no clue how to buy them though. It was computer code you were buying. There was no exchange, nothing I could find, computer geeks only.

I tried two of my friends. One was an airline pilot the other a software assurance specialist. Both pretty bright and as computer-literate as I knew. Never heard of it, they said. Look into it, I said. They never got back to me.

I let it slip, got on with my day job. They took off a bit, over the following years. By the time we had moved to the States and had cashed out of our home and stables in the UK, they had hit $50 each. My few hundred pounds would have grown to around $2.5 million.

That's annoying, I thought. I toyed with buying $5,000 worth. But that's only a hundred bitcoins.... I could have had 40,000 for that few hundred pounds. I left it.

On December 17, 2017, not a day I look back on with fondness, bitcoin reached an all-time high of $19,783 dollars. Do you want me to do the math? Of course you do. My three hundred pounds of bitcoins would have been worth around $794 million.

That's it really. Not much else to say. There isn't anything you can say is there.

No, Oh well.... it's only money....there's always tomorrow. No, not really. It's a conversation stopper. The king of conversation stoppers. As the realization of how sometimes one small action can make such a difference.

And that is the point my friends. IF I had made that bet. Bill Gates made the bet. So did Jeff Bezos. So did Steve Jobs. I went out and made my bet on two dirt cheap unbroken yearlings and scraped a living for twenty years out of my bet. And got some fantastic days and memories out of it. That was the bet I made.

Bitcoin was the one I didn't. So don't feel sorry for me. Or for anyone who didn't make the bet. Who never made the bet. Who never took a chance. Never took the plunge, so don't deserve any reward.

So, you see, I feel sorry for the guy I saw on the news around the time bitcoin fever was at its highest. I saw him scrambling around on his hands and knees in the biggest junk pile you have ever seen.

He was a needle in a haystack – looking for the needle in the haystack that was his old computer that he had thrown out. With what now, he realized, was $12 million dollars of bitcoins on his hard drive.

What a schmuck.

On October 15, 2021 bitcoin hit an all time high of $60,883. Don't say a thing.

CHAPTER 29

Clothes Maketh the Man

I'll tell you what I can't get used to about the States. Classlessness. People dress the same here. What is it with that? I can't tell who anyone is over here. You can tell a lot about people by how they dress in the UK. Not here. That means I keep putting my foot in it.

I can't tell you the amount of times I would return from a set to our barn, there is some guy I haven't seen before stood around with a belly a baseball cap and a ten-dollar T shirt. I breeze past, tell him we are good for hotwalkers today thanks, and then Kenny walks up to him and greets him warmly, and I find out later this is one of our biggest owners who happened (more by luck than anything else I would say judging by that T shirt) to start a company from scratch and sell it for two hundred million dollars. And then he did it all over again (how does a guy get that lucky)?

If someone had even a fraction of that money back in the UK, they are going to let everyone know. They will arrive to see their trainer by helicopter and will step out wearing more labels than a black Jewish transgender dwarf. Poor people would be forced to lay in puddles so they can walk over them to keep their designer footwear clean. And if they pay for something, they won't pull out some generic credit card. No. They will pull out their diamond encrusted granite credit card that has been pressed to the breast of a virgin and farted on by Warren Buffet himself.

You see, I would like to start training again. So, I need to find owners. But how do I know who to talk to? I don't want to find myself spending half an afternoon at the sales chatting up some old guy dressed like a hotwalker, only to discover he is actually a hotwalker.

I didn't have that problem back in Newmarket. There were sometimes imposters. People who would dress like they were someone they weren't. But most of the time people knew what uniform they were supposed to wear.

Posh kids have floppy hair. Poor kids have gel in their hair. Steeplechase trainers wear tweed, and so do their owners. Flat trainers wear suits, flat owners wear a thawb and keffiyeh. Stable staff wear breeches and polo shirts. Except for Gordon. Or Geordie as he was known around town. Geordie worked for Sir Mark Prescott. He was from Newcastle and spoke with a dialect so acutely garbled that not even other Geordies had any idea what he was talking about. He was a jockey back in the day. He got a contract with an Arab sheik to ride in Saudi Arabia one winter, him and his wife went. The sheik decided to keep his wife. So, when Geordie returned alone back to Newmarket he decided to become an alcoholic. He was very good at it. He would wander from pub to pub each evening wearing his Newcastle United football shirt, he would talk to everyone in every pub at some point each evening. You would just nod your head occasionally, say "Yes Geordie" "ok" "I see" and then he would move on. Someone would find him later laid somewhere around town asleep and help him back to Sir Mark's lodgings. I helped him home a couple of times (he may even have repaid the favour once I believe).

Everyone has their role in the UK, everyone knows their place, their part. Who they are supposed to be. You don't get educated at Harrow and walk around in a football shirt. You wear a football shirt if you come from the part of town that beats up people who went to Harrow if they come across one.

I just don't know in America. I can't judge the book by the cover here. I have to try and get to know the person. At the start of the Spring meet at Keeneland some guy showed up at the barn, he had a twinkle in his eye and was dressed so scruffily that I thought this man must be a billionaire at least! So, I treated him with deference, joked with him, gave him a seat in the office, and made friends with him. Turned out he was a hotwalker. So, I gave him a job. We stayed pals. I still secretly believe he is a billionaire though.

CHAPTER 30

Glass Half Full

Optimists tend to be wrong more often than pessimists. However, optimists tend to be happier than pessimists. It seems it is better to go through life in ignorant bliss, and perhaps just receive a nasty shock right at the end, than to correctly predict the whole world is heading to hell in a hand basket – or whatever the saying is.

I like to think of myself as a realist, but more and more lately it seems hard to separate a realist from a pessimist, just as it is increasingly difficult lately to distinguish the difference between an optimist and a raving lunatic.

I am going to give it a go though. It is a new year. Now, I'm not saying that I got an uncomfortable feeling last New Year's Eve when everyone was high fiving and whooping about 2020. How this was going to be THE year!!! But I did. Well they were right, it was THE year, just not in the way they expected.

I don't think 2021 is going to be much to whoop about either, with climate change still there lurking behind the dread fog of Covid.

Standing on the cusp of a possible economic black swan. We may find that 2020 was the beginning of a new reality. That this time they really were the good old days, those past decades.

But I am going to be an optimist for once, I am going to ignore all the facts, the data, human nature, all the dinosaur bones, and deliver an upbeat message through the medium of horseracing. Because in 2020 this declining, ever-less-relevant industry (in most people's eyes anyway) delivered us diversion, entertainment, excitement and – perhaps most importantly – days to look forward to. And that is something to really be happy about.

Horseracing people are a tough bunch, the riders especially, but also the grooms, hot walkers, and the trainers who have to take the financial risk entering such a competitive business.

The tough people within the industry carried on, business as usual. The best thing of course. Who wouldn't want to? So many couldn't, but they could, and they did and we were treated to Tiz The Law as a starter, Authentic as main course, and Swiss Skydiver for dessert. The Travers, the Derby, the Preakness, the Classic. For a while you forgot about everything else and cheered them home.

It is a dangerous but beautiful sport, horseracing. A bit like life. An analogy to life. Life is exciting, beautiful, but can suddenly without warning turn ugly, turn chaotic. Eventually, though, the sun comes out again.

And so it goes, the world keeps turning, another race is run, Thoroughbred racing has kept going for 400 years now. The great, the humble, the famous, the anonymous, the fabulously wealthy and the equally fabulously poor, bound together by a love of the horse.

They really are the stars of the show, of the industry. Whenever this sport reaches the mainstream (for good reasons), whenever it captures the public's imagination and heart, it is because of the horses. Seabiscuit, Secretariat, American Pharaoh, Arkle, Desert Orchid, Enable.

It is, when you cut everything else away, about beautiful horses, one of the things coveted most by wealthy men for millennia. Wealthy men one day began matching their finest specimens against each other. And then came the masses to watch the first real sport, and then to bet on it. Gentleman betting amounts back then that would make a high roller swoon now. Working men pressing coins into each other's hands, raising the adrenaline, raising the stakes, eyes straining for their silks.

It is a beautiful spectacle, a thrilling spectacle, a wonderful sport, as it is a wonderful life. The race may be run, but the sport continues into the future, as it emerged from the past, fully drawn for our generation.

The history of the sport is so rich, the people, the famous races, the horses, the stories intertwined with the history of nations, of the world, so much of it recorded, captured. Go to the Keeneland Library, when times change, and see the archives, the depth of coverage of the *Sport of Kings* way back then. No other sport even comes close to the romance of that, to the way it has emerged from history.

Of course, the players of today shall not be the players of tomorrow. They will change, but the sport hopefully will continue. We have a duty to look after it and pass it on, if we can, better than we received it. All we have to do to achieve that is take good care of the brave competitors.

If we look after and love the Thoroughbreds who do our bidding and race for us, then the rest shall take care of itself.

If we polish them and show people we love those shiny Thoroughbreds, and tell their story, then how can some people not fall in love with the whole thing and become fans of the sport themselves.

When people visit Saratoga or Keeneland for the first time, they must find it beautiful. If they encounter the horse farms around Lexington and see the foals playing in the paddocks, how can they not be amazed? If they attend an auction and take in the show and drama, a Thoroughbred yearling sleek under spotlights, the mindboggling sums changing hands against the auctioneers machine-gun patter, how can they not be in awe?

Horseracing represents the beauty of nature. The Thoroughbred is perhaps the most beautiful of a beautiful species, powerful, volatile, steaming, snorting, and fast. So fast.

Horseracing represents life, procreation, the struggle to life, survival of the fittest, sometimes red in claw, sometimes the wild celebration of a tribe's victory in battle. Again and again, battle after battle, until the champion emerges, the champions, the kings and the queens. And they will be paired and mate, as they would in nature.

So, in a time of uncertainty, of a pandemic, a time of fake media (does anyone even know for sure who the president is yet?), in a time when hundreds of thousands, maybe millions of people, are finding their jobs, maybe their whole industry sector, under threat, collapsing, dying out, like dinosaurs after the meteorite struck, completely unexpected, out of the blue, from nowhere, in this time it looks as if, fortunately for us, the Thoroughbred industry shall survive. The sport can continue, the betting, the cheering, the anticipation can continue. The breeders, owners, trainers can continue, employment for the horsemen can continue.

We are very lucky, very lucky. Who would have guessed that the sport, no longer in the public eye, would prove so resilient, so robust?

Perhaps all we have to do for the sport of horseracing to survive and thrive, is just take care of the beautiful Thoroughbreds that are at the centre of it all. Perhaps all we have to do is treat them with respect. Maybe all we have to do is show how we love them, for other people to grow to love the sport also. We are very lucky if that is all we have to do to carry on having a good life.The glass is more than half full, let's not spill anything.

CHAPTER 31

Sir Mark Prescott

I was neighbors with Sir Mark Prescott for the best part of 16 years. On the first morning I encountered him, I said, "Good morning, Sir Mark." He replied "Good morning Mr Gilligan." Sixteen years later, on my last morning in Newmarket, I said, "Good morning, Sir Mark." And he said, "Good morning, Mr Gilligan.

I sent my son to Heath House, for his apprenticeship. If you cannot afford to send your child to public school, you should consider Heath House.

Jack looks back with fondness on those times, making friends, laughing with his fellow workers, sitting the tough ones. It toughened him up and gave him a seat on a horse a prince would be proud of. He still hasn't thanked me.

Everything is as it should be with Sir Mark. Within the ivy covered walls of his Heath House stables, superficially at least, time stands still. Evening stables inspections are conducted with a formality found nowhere else anymore. The legendary but tragic jockey Fred Archer was apprenticed to trainer Matt Dawson here and, despite the addition of equine treadmills, pools, horse walkers and other state of the art training aids, the place still seemingly breaths Victorian fog from its chimneys.

Sir Mark says he does have a mobile phone – but no-one has the number.

He inherited his Baronetcy in 1965, and by 1970, following an 18-month stay in hospital after a fall in a steeplechase broke his back, he became Newmarket's newest, and youngest (by 19 years) racehorse trainer.

For many years never seen without a cigar in his hand, Sir Mark Prescott has lived his life on his terms. The old Harrovian has lived a Sherlock Holmesian lifestyle, a confirmed bachelor in spite of his enjoyment of female companionship, with a love of the arts and horse racing history and the entry book.

He has landed legendary gambles and improbable winning sequences that have left the handicappers scratching their heads. In 1980, he trained 2-year-old Spindrifter to 13 victories in a season, the first time it had been done in 100 years. In 2004, he wrung seven victories from three-year-old Masafi – in 12 days, at six different racecourses, covering 2,500 miles by horse box.

He is the longest-serving trainer in Britain now, teetotal, and much too sprightly for his assistant's liking. This son of a barrister has spent his life turning the training of a racehorse into a piece of performance art.

He has played the part of Newmarket trainer for five decades now, and, with the sad passing of the equally iconic Sir Henry Cecil, Prescott stands head and shoulders above all others now as an emblem of Newmarket, the sport of kings, and actually England too, now I think about it.

If you have never met him, it is your loss, but you are not alone. He has turned away some of the biggest names in the sport who came and sought his services – not for personal reasons, it is just that he has 50 stables, and he trains 50 horses, year-in, year-out. Not one less, not one more.

Who do you think is the most important person in world racing history?

Admiral Henry John Rous (1791-1877), the great British racing administrator who invented and perfected the weight-for-age scale, which is virtually unchanged to this day, and on which all races and handicaps throughout the world are framed.

(One of Prescott's favorite stories has Admiral Rous one day climbing the Newmarket grandstand steps when a lady exclaims, "Why Admiral Rous, you seem very cheery today, may I ask why?" "Well Madame," he replies. "I have just gone through the next race and have discovered that I have handicapped each horse so well, that not one of them can possibly win.")

What is your favourite race and venue?

My favourite race is the Melbourne Cup. The atmosphere in the city for the ten days leading up to it is unique.

The venue is Epsom Racecourse. Anyone who hasn't visited the home of the Derby should climb to the top of the grandstand. The view across the hills of Surrey, from that vantage point high on the top of the downs, is spectacular.

From there it is easy to see why Federico Tesio regarded the Derby at Epsom as the supreme test of a Thoroughbred in the world.

The winning horse, only a 3-year-old in June, had to survive fast ground (over a mile and a half) and, in Tesio's time, a crowd of a million. The horse's temperament had to withstand a parade, a canter down, a canter back and a long walk across the downs to the start.

He had to gallop uphill and downhill and, in the latter stages, cope with a pronounced camber.

He had to turn right-handed and left-handed. He had to have the pace to secure an early position, but a disposition that allowed him to settle in mid race, plus the acceleration and stamina to climb the final hill.

On a raceday, or on a quiet day for that matter, racing history suffuses the whole place and any ardent lover of the turf could seek no finer view.

What is your fondest memory in racing?

Riding my first winner, at my first ever attempt, aged 16 at Wincanton Racecourse on September 17, 1964, in a 2-mile steeplechase. One never forgets one's first kiss. However many more may follow, there is only one first kiss!

What do you see as the biggest challenge racing faces today?

Welfare. In an increasingly urban world, more and more people believe that animals think like humans, while fewer and fewer people learn enough about animals to know how they think!

Thus our administrators have a hard job on their hands. Modern people know about pets, watch enough wildlife programs to comprehend the wild, but have no experience or understanding of the working animal anymore, and that is our greatest challenge.

If you could change one thing in racing, what would it be?

I would try to ensure that those in control of the sport continue to contain an element of sportsmen and sportswomen and those with a love and deep knowledge of animals. Bureaucrats have a place, but should not dominate.

CHAPTER 32

Simon & Haynie's Maria

He was said to have been just four feet and six inches tall and possessed of very long arms and legs, a small body and a hunchback.

He came to South Carolina on a slave ship from Africa when just a child. Some said he was a Prince in his homeland. He became a Prince of the American turf. A future president of the USA tried to defeat him nine times. And nine times he failed.

He was thought to have been born in the early 1780s, and turned into a slave around the age of ten. It is not known if he had encountered horses before arriving – rather unexpectedly – in the newly formed United States, where horseracing in South Carolina was pre-eminent and already well established.

As a teenager, he rode against the best. Apparently, he had an aloof manner, possessed great wit and a strong line in sarcasm. He was described at the time as a most skillful jockey with a graceful seat and no danger, no peril too great for his courage. He didn't seem to have read the label placed upon him, and in truth it mattered not upon a horse in the heat of a race, black and white faces were equal there between the rails.

While post war anti-English sentiment and puritanism saw racing fade in the North, it continued to thrive in the South.

He became famous in South Carolina, and although he had nicknames, those with bearing on the track, with unexpected respect, invariably just referred to him as Simon.

He was owned by a man called Foster but was often rented out to a Colonel George Elliott, who raced in Tennessee. The Prince would have seen the newly introduced Irish bluegrass there, before it ever blew into Kentucky.

One time Simon was riding against one of Elliot's horses. Simon won the race by employing every form of jockeyship he had in his arsenal and cost the Colonel $1,000 in lost wagers. The Colonel's temper lost, he tore a strip off the four-foot-six slave for his tactics. The Prince coolly returned, "Well Colonel Elliot, I've won many a race that way for you, and it is the first time I ever heard you object."

General Andrew Jackson was prominent in the forming of the Nashville racecourse and indeed the whole sport in Tennessee.

A formidable man, a sturdy six feet one, and a temper to go with it, he once dueled a man over an unpaid forfeit for a race (could it have been at the Dueling Grounds – now Kentucky Downs?) He aimed deliberately at the man's groin, and didn't miss, fatally wounding him. Simon, though, it seemed, looked down on him. What is a Major General compared with a Prince?

Her name was Maria. She was a daughter of Diomed, the recently imported winner of the very first English Derby. She was owned by a Captain Jesse Haynie and became known as Haynie's Maria.

Maria and the Prince defeated the General in battle after battle. In the end, the General had to wave the white flag. He retired from the challenge in bad spirit, and went off to do something less challenging – like running the country. He would go on to set up a full racing stables at the White House. That is what a big deal horseracing was back then.

Maria and the Prince defeated Jackson's charge a couple of times, and Jackson didn't like it one bit. He embarked on grudge match after grudge match, and each time the Prince swatted him away, leaving Jackson beetroot red.

Before one contest, Jackson approached the rider and said, "Now Simon, when my horse and rider come to pass you, don't spit your tobacco juice in their eyes."

"Why General," the Prince replied, "I rode a great deal against your horses, but none of them ever got close enough to catch my spit." Jackson was defeated again.

Jackson swore he would beat Haynie's Maria – if a horse could just be found in the United States to do it!

After their ninth and final battle, Jackson apparently "became like a madman, sending forth bitter oaths and torrents of threats".

The Prince looked on in amusement.

Simon was a fine banjo player, and sang amusing made-up ditties. He came across Major General Andrew Jackson one day in a crowd. And this he said or sang to the warrior general:

"General, you were always ugly, but now you're a show, I could make a fortune by showing you as you now look, If I had you in a cage where you could not hurt the people who come to look."

The Prince, still enslaved, still rented out, took umbrage one year when his master tried to bid him up. Concerned he would lose the employment of his favored choice of retainer, he turned to Colonel Foster and said, "By God, I'm not a selling, just hired for one year."

This infuriated Foster, who replied, "You impudent scoundrel! Do you know who you are talking to?!"

"I think I do." The Prince replied. "If I am not mistaken, you are the same gentleman who made a failed experiment for Governor once."

Haynie's Maria tasted defeated only once, in her final race, at the age of nine.

"Was there ever anything you ever undertook heartily and failed to accomplish?" An older General Jackson was asked once.

"Not that I can remember," he replied. "Except Haynie's Maria. I could not beat her."

Or the Prince. General Jackson couldn't beat the Prince either. The Prince of American horseracing, in his own mind at least.

The Prince died of cholera in Tennessee in 1833. His death was reported in Nashville's *National Banner*:

DEATHS IN NASHVILLE BY CHOLERA

Simon, negro man, commonly called Monkey Simon, aged 52.

He wasn't labelled as a slave, though, so maybe he died free at least.

CHAPTER 33

Danny Ramsey

He is an ordained minister who shared a joint with Bob Marley back in the day. He is a black belt in Karate and sports a six pack. He doesn't drink alcohol or soda or eat fried food. He is a loving husband to Eleanor and father to five children, Danist, Marcus, Tamara, Domanick and Lance. He has 13 grandchildren and two great grandchildren.

Danny Ramsey was born in Nassau in the Bahamas, and that is where he encountered his first racehorse.

It might seem like he has led a charmed life, but not really. He is just indomitable.

His father died when he was just 7, and his mother passed within a year of her husband. He said it hit him very hard, his mother's death.

He was sent to live with his older brother, who was mean to him and beat the small boy.

He introduced him to horses, though, and gave him a harsh tuition. But tuition it was nonetheless, and young Danny took his lessons seriously.

He rode his first race age 16 and soon became leading apprentice in his native country. He was riding out in the post parade one day when he saw a young girl standing under a tree. He asked the outrider who she was and was told she was the sister of the owner of the horse he was riding. That was a problem, as the 'deal' was on, and he was supposed to let some 10/1 shot win.

"The deal's off!" he exclaimed to the consternation of the outrider. One of the conspirators approached him behind the gate and pleaded with him, but Danny said, "No, the deal is off!" And he won the race. In the winner's enclosure, he said, "Tell your sister I'm in love with her."

At the age of 19 he moved to the States with his young wife.

He race-rode for a while, but then took a bad fall and became a full-time exercise rider for Albert Winick, until Winick passed 26 years later. He said he became like a father to him and was heartbroken at his death.

After a brief stint training a small string of cheap horses, Danny joined John Ward and stayed with him until Ward's retirement. He still tells stories of riding the truculent and temperamental Fusaichi Pegasus, who was with Ward initially before joining Neil Drysdale, who trained him to win the 2000 Kentucky Derby.

In 2012, Danny was headhunted by Kenny McPeek. Just three employers over all those years. A testament to his skill and loyalty.

That is where I met him, when I worked as Kenny's assistant for the best part of two years. Danny was the person who made me laugh again, made me start to love life again.

His positivity and humor are infectious. I would be leading one of his horses to the track, and he would pass riders and they would ask him how he was. "I'm good. I'm better than good!" he would exclaim. "if you're doing better than me I must be dead, so put me in the ground!" And he would start laughing to himself and so would I. And he said this most days, and still every day we laughed together.

We stood together and hugged in the winner's enclosure at Saratoga as Eskimo Kisses flew past the wire in front in the G1 Alabama Stakes in 2018. That race is still one of my best memories in racing. A lot of people leave racing with little, but those memories, what price could you put on them though?

Ramsey was Eskimo Kisses' regular rider, as he had been with Restless Rider when she won the G1 Alcibiades at Keeneland that spring.

He was breezing a horse at Gulfstream one morning in March 2020. A big heavy horse. Its bandage came undone, the big heavy horse tripped on it and came down. They were both fired into the dirt. The outrider thought Danny was dead when he reached him. He obviously didn't know Danny very well.

He was badly hurt, though, a broken collarbone, broken jaw, cracked spine and severe concussion. I spoke to him weeks later. And then again months later and found he was not back at work yet. He had played down the seriousness of his injuries to me initially. I hoped he would be okay, wouldn't get sick with anything else while recuperating. That wouldn't be good. I hoped for his wife's sake that he could be mobile and alright in his retirement.

When I heard a few months later that he was riding out again, I thought my ears might fall off.

Muhammed Ali, one of my other heroes, made one of the greatest comebacks in history in the *Rumble In the Jungle*, in what was known as Zaire in 1974 against the heavy hitting, seemingly invincible George Foreman.

Professional commentators worried about Ali, the hopeless outsider, that he could get seriously hurt. But Ali's charm, his wit, his humanity won over the people of the what is now the Democratic Republic of the Congo. The children would run with him and he would stop and play-spar with them and they would all be laughing, amazed at the giant man.

The man who became one of the great icons of human history would stop to play with children when training for his greatest battle. And all the while the people looked on and would cheer in the Bantu language Lingala, "Ali Boom Ba Ye! Ali Boom Ba Ye!" *(Ali, kill him! Ali kill him!).* Sixty thousand people were there that night and watched Ali 'kill' him.

Danny's comeback was greater than that, though.

He is 70 years of age, Danny Ramsey, and each morning now he goes to the track and he gallops Swiss Skydiver.

He's been killing it for years.

Danny, Bom Ba Ye. Danny, Bom Ba Ye

CHAPTER 34

Preakness & The Woodlawn Vase

Woodlawn Racecourse was formed by the Woodlawn Racing Association in Louisville in 1858. It held its first race meet in the fall of the following year, a full 16 years before Churchill Downs would stage its first race.

The initial meets proved a success. The racecourse was popularly considered one of the best anywhere, and the great and the good came both to see the sports and to be seen.

By 1862, however, the Civil War impacted Woodlawn Racecourse to such an extent that one of the officers of the track, Robert Alexander, an eminent Thoroughbred breeder, buried on his horse farm for safekeeping a magnificent sporting challenge trophy he had commissioned just two years earlier.

After the war, Woodlawn never recovered its initial popularity. By 1870, it had staged its last race.

The Woodlawn Vase, as the buried trophy was known, was thereafter posted by different owners for different races at different tracks. By 1878, it had emigrated east to New Jersey, and from there to Jerome Park, and then Morris Park racetrack in New York.

Eventually, in 1917, it arrived at Pimlico Racecourse, where it was put up as the trophy awarded to the winner of the Preakness Stakes.

The trophy was awarded annually to winning connections until 1953. Nowdays, a one-third-size trophy goes to the winning owner, and smaller replicas still go to the winning trainer and jockey. They are still made of sterling silver, though, and the owner gets to keep it. Each replica Woodlawn Vase is valued at $40,000.

That is why the original trophy is no longer awarded as a challenge trophy as it once was, entrusted to each winning owner for 12 months until the following year's contest.

The actual Woodlawn Vase stands three feet high. It is formed from 30lbs of solid sterling silver. On top of the base stands a stallion and a mare and foal. Above that is inscribed the rules for competing for the Woodlawn Vase. Above that, on the main body of the bowl, are four shields. Two are blank, one has a representation of a racehorse, and the other a representation of Woodlawn Racecourse. Higher up are four figures of victory, a wreath held in their outstretched arms. Above that are portraits of the eight officers of the Woodlawn Racecourse Association.

Finally, the whole piece is topped by a sculpture of a famous racehorse and great sire of the day. More of him later.

The original trophy, when commissioned by Robert Alexander, cost $1,000. Tiffany's, the world-famous jewelers, were engaged to create it. It was a shrewd commission.

Indeed, the Preakness winner's check wouldn't buy the trophy that represents the race. Justify, who in 2018 won all three legs of the Triple Crown, earned just under $3 million for his efforts. Even that wouldn't be enough to buy the Woodlawn Vase.

It is, in fact, estimated to be the most valuable sporting trophy in North America, and the second most valuable sporting trophy in the world today. (The FIFA World Cup, made of 18 carat gold, is the only one valued higher). I know though, if I was an American billionaire, which of those trophies I would covet more.

Preakness was foaled in 1867 in Kentucky, and sold there as a yearling for $2,000, the highest price noted for a Thoroughbred yearling at that time.

He was purchased by prominent owner M H Sanford and was named after his own Preakness Stud in Preakness, New Jersey.

He was a great racehorse of his time, winning 18 of his 39 starts. On his first start, he won the inaugural running of the 2-mile Dinner Party Stakes, the second richest stakes ever run in the United States at that time, at the newly formed Pimlico racecourse.

Later he was exported to England to race. He finished second in a handicap at Epsom Downs and was subsequently sold to stand at stud there.

He was shot dead one day in 1881 by his new owner, the Duke of Hamilton. Apparently both horse and owner had temperament issues.

The greatest stallion of his day was Lexington. He stood at Woodburn Farm, perhaps the most important historic horse farm in North American Thoroughbred racing history.

Woodburn Farm was owned by Robert Alexander, the man who commissioned Tiffany's to create the Woodlawn Vase, which he buried at his farm all those years ago. It was the same farm where Preakness was born.

The famous stallion standing atop the trophy is Lexington. He became one of the greatest sires of all time. And he was the father of Preakness.

Today the vase is on display at the Baltimore Museum of Art. Each year it is brought to Pimlico in May, on Preakness Stakes day, by the Maryland National Guard.

If you get a chance to see it at Pimlico, or at the Baltimore Museum of Art, you should take it. It is a piece of American history, and of American art. And you will get to see what $4 million looks like.

If you ever drive past Airdrie Stud Farm on Frankfort Pike in Lexington, Kentucky, then you are passing Woodburn Farm, where treasure was once buried, and treasure was once born.

CHAPTER 35

Old Friends

I wanted to look into the welfare of ex-racehorses – to find out about retirement homes and rehabilitation programs, to understand what was out there – and how much or little of it there was. Since Old Friends was just 15 minutes down the road in Georgetown, Kentucky, that seemed like a good place to start.

I was greeted by 74-year-old Michael Blowen putting a miniature pony into a small paddock next to the office. Blowen, who founded Old Friends in 2003, let me take a couple of pictures of *Little Silver Charm* and then took me for a gentle walk around his farm and told me his story.

"I only got involved in all this because I liked drinking and gambling! I didn't fall in love with the horses until later. I've got a horse here I claimed from Finger Lakes in 1999 for $3,500."

The first horse he introduced me to was Birdstone. "The world's most hated Belmont winner! I was there when he beat Smarty Jones [bidding to complete the Triple Crown in 2004]. He's a little nutty," says Blowen.

He introduced me to Sun King, who earned around $2 million on the track and was fourth in the 2005 Preakness. He and Birdstone were both trained by Nick Zito.

I ask Blowen who the oldest horse they have here is. You And I, he says. He is 30, and they have the oldest living Breeders' Cup Classic winner here also, Alphabet Soup, who is just 44 days younger.

"I wanted to specialize in taking stallions," says Blowen. "No one else was taking them and I thought, well they are the stars and I know people like to see the stars. I was one of those people, the first time I stepped foot in Kentucky, the first thing I did was go see Bold Forbes and Forego at the Kentucky Horse Park."

"We started with 52 acres, bought 44 more, and now we have 236 acres. There are a lot of places now rehoming and retraining retired racehorses, aided by Thoroughbred Aftercare Alliance, who do a great job."

"Hey, Silver Charm!" He calls across the paddock to an old gray with a long silver mane. "You gonna come say hello buddy?" The Hall of Famer, winner of the Kentucky Derby and Preakness in 1997 and the Dubai World Cup a year later, lifts his head and starts walking towards us and then he breaks into a jog to come say hello to his old friend. We spend a bit of time there and I watch them make a fuss of each other.

"He's my favorite horse of all time," Blowen says quietly. "27 years old now."

"We've brought seven stallions home from Japan. Japanese Racing Authority representatives visited them. Now they have set up their own facility over there. It's going to be fantastic. They wanted to call it Old Friends."

Blowen introduces me to Alphabet Soup, an aging gray in a clean airy stall with his companion donkey *Gorgeous George* by his side. He's 30 years old now, an old man.

"He survived cancer," Blowen tells me as he scratches the horse's back. "He won the Breeders' Cup Classic in 1996 at Woodbine. Chris McCarron rode him. The donkey follows him everywhere. Just walks out to the paddock behind him."

We discuss aftercare and funding. "It's unbelievable that there's nothing organized within the industry here for the athletes, the horses and the jockeys," he says. "That after their careers there is nothing for them. It's all piecemeal.

"If just a little bit was taken off each transaction, they could be looked after."

Nearby is a graveyard in the shape of a horseshoe. There are some famous names there who saw their days out in tranquil bliss after serving the sport so well.

And it's not charity. These retired old horses are some of the best marketing tools the sport has – these happy relaxed old stars, and old claimers, in this pretty quiet setting. Around 20,000 people a year come to Old Friends in Kentucky to see former champions of the Turf, to pet some modest old claimer.

"We have Hogy [winner of 19 races, including three G3s] and Soi Phet [15 victories]. They are both millionaires who retired at 11 completely sound. They were looked after, were given time off each winter.

"If people thought these horses in racing were really being well looked after, they would beat a path to the sport.

"Green Mask is one of my favorites. He broke his leg but the owner loved him and paid for it to be fixed. Eventually with the aftercare, he couldn't afford it anymore and they sent him to us. We sent him to Kesmarc, a great facility, for rehabilitation. Sallee Vans took him each time, neither of them ever sent us a bill. Dr Waldridge, our vet for the past six years, has never sent us a bill."

Green Mask is happy in his paddock at Old Friends, and he runs up to Blowen when he calls him by name, even with his gammy-looking front leg.

Blowen spoke of "legendary veterinarian" Dr Doug Bayers. "He never sent us a bill either," he says. "We named our lane there after him, Bayer's Way. We joke it's Bayer's way or the highway.

"I asked him one day whether he would help me because I didn't know what the hell I was doing. I asked if he would be my vet if I promised not to go calling him at two in the morning. He looked at me, leant back and put his legs up on his desk and said he would only become my vet on one condition. That I *would* call him at two in the morning. He taught me so much."

Old Friends has 126 horses now, and around 20,000 visitors a year. "Antonio Marin is my head man for the horses," says Blowen. "He is great. Without his help, I wouldn't sleep at night."

Blowen calls out each horse by name. "Summer! Summer! What are you doing buddy!" He talks to the horses all the time. We saw The Pizza Man, a $2million-plus earner whose 17 wins include the 2015 Arlington Million, and 2014 Breeders' Cup Sprint hero Work All Week. Every horse I saw was in a fine paddock, with an equally fine field shelter. Every one was happy and relaxed. This place is good for the soul. If you are ever feeling jaded with the world, come here and you will leave feeling better.

"We got our first big stallion, [1990 Big Cap winner] Ruhlmann, from Jerry Moss. Bobby Frankel had trained him for a year [1988].

I went over to him one day at Saratoga and I told him we had his horse. He said, that's nice and walked away. Two days later, he taps me on the shoulder and says aren't you that guy with Ruhlmann, and he spoke with me at length and was great.

"A couple months after he passed away, we found he had left us a very substantial contribution. We were blown way. Not long after that, we were receiving box after box onto the farm, he left us nearly every one of his trophies too.

"I was a movie critic for the *Boston Globe* and my wife, Diane White, was a columnist. So, one year I was coming back from the Saratoga meet and I had made money, had a great time and was full of myself. I was convinced that this year I was going to win the *Boston Magazine* award for best movie critic – because everyone else had left! David Ansen, Janet Maslin, and another guy went to the *New Yorker* – they had to give it to me!

"So I get the magazine from the news stand and the headline reads Diane White is like Snow White and all the other columnists are like the dwarves – especially her husband, Dopey!"

I don't think Michael Blowen is Dopey and, anyway, wasn't Dopey Snow White's favorite? But I think he is good-hearted and maybe a bit soft-hearted and what he does touches people when they visit.

Still though, it has been a struggle at times.

Blowen told me that a year and a half ago they were in the worst shape they had been in, about $100,000 in debt. It was coming up to Halloween. Blowen thought he would try to hang on until closer to Christmas before approaching his bank, hoping for some seasonal goodwill from them.

He had done three tours this day, and was sitting by Silver Charm's paddock enjoying a well-earned beer when he heard a car pull in. He went down to meet it and a nice younger couple said they had heard about Old Friends and wanted to pay it a visit. He asked them if they could come back the next day as they were now closed, but they said they couldn't. They were heading back to Fargo North Dakota the following morning.

Blowen relented, gave them each a beer and told them to hop in the golf buggy for a guided tour.

Afterwards, when Blowen dropped the couple back at their car, the man said they had really enjoyed the tour and that he wanted to make a donation but had forgotten his check book. Michael had heard that one in 18 different languages and thought no more of it.

A couple of weeks passed and then one day the man called him and said he was going to send him a check.

It was the morning after Thanksgiving, Blowen walked to his letterbox as he did daily, wondering whether there would be some checks, or just more bills.

There was only one envelope in there this day. It was from Fargo North Dakota. There was no letter inside, no message, just a check for half a million dollars.

CHAPTER 36
Adam Kirby

The Epsom Derby, the original Derby, is the daddy of them all. First run in 1780, 95 years before the first Kentucky Derby, it became known as 'the Blue Riband of the Turf'. In its heyday, half a million people would cover Epsom Downs, the country would stop, virtually every man, woman and child in Britain would have a small flutter on the Derby.

Legend has it that the name was decided on a coin toss between the Earl of Derby and Sir Charles Bunbury. Bunbury may have lost the toss, but he won the first running with Diomed, who in later years became a successful sire in the recently formed United States of America.

Jockey Adam Kirby recently rode Adayar to victory in the Derby for Godolphin. It was a huge moment for the well-liked 32-year-old rider, whom I remember as a kid but is now partner of Megan and father of 5-year-old Charlie and 3-year-old Evie.

I knew Adam's father, Maurice. He had a small farm outside Newmarket and a couple of horses in a shared barn we rented when

I first arrived in town with two cheap yearlings and about £50 in my back pocket.

Maurice employed a small Welsh stable hand, known as Taffy, to train and exercise his horses. I remember Taffy one day asked Maurice for a new broom to sweep the yard. A couple of days later, I came into the barn to find Taffy wandering around the place chortling and showing everyone the small plastic kitchen broom Maurice had purchased for him. Maurice knew the value of a pound, and he had a sense of humor.

Adam Kirby hated school, so at age 12 he quit, and started riding out full-time for a local trainer. As soon as he turned 16, another Newmarket trainer, Michael Wigham, took his licence out for him.

"Michael was a great tutor, and a top man, but it was Gay Kelleway who gave me my first ride and that was my first winner," says Kirby.

Maurice would drive his son to the races in the early days and some of Adam's earliest winners were for me. The first winner he rode for me was a little filly called Avit, in a lowly claimer. Neither of us were the tidiest or most fashion-conscious individuals and, Adam Kirby and I could be seen sporting Covid hairstyles around the racecourses of Britain well over a decade before Covid hair was even a thing.

A day or two after winning on Avit we were riding back home together after training on the heath. Sir Mark Prescott was standing waiting for his horses to come round, so I thought I would give the aspiring young jockey a plug. I said good morning, pointed to Adam and said, "This is the young apprentice who won on mine the other day, Sir Mark."

Prescott took a look at Kirby, pulled his cigar out of his mouth and said, "Well its got F-all to do with the jockeys has it!"

Young Kirby didn't let that encounter throw him off his stride, and the trickle of winners soon turned into a stream.

"I finished second twice in the apprentice championship," he says. "Luckily, after losing my weight allowance, things kept going and I built up a link with Walter Swinburn and then Clive Cox, who started to give me quality horses in bigger races."

Kirby's career continued on a gentle upward trajectory. He had to miss his first-born's birth to ride a G1 winner on Profitable at Royal Ascot in 2016 and won a few more at the top level in the years since, but he had yet to taste glory in one of the Classics.

"I was asked to ride John Leeper in the Derby this year, which was great," he says. "But then Frankie [Dettori] came available, so I lost the ride. Then Charlie [Appleby, Godolphin trainer] called me and said I could ride Adayar.

"I break Charlie's yearlings in at our farm and actually broke in Adayar as a yearling. That was the last time I sat on him before I rode him in the Derby. He was lovely and laid back.

"I was pretty laid back about the race. He'd run in the trials and it was just nice to pick up a ride in a race like that. Charlie is a top man and a gentleman and we get on very well, and he is an excellent trainer and a nice person, which counts for a lot. I'd gone out to Dubai a couple of times and rode a couple of winners for Charlie there as well, which was great."

Adayar had to work fairly hard early on in the Derby. "I had to use a bit of petrol the first furlong and a half to get a good position," says Kirby. "But from there on it went very smooth he took me into the straight lovely, and luckily we found a gap on the inside. I had a lovely position throughout and he always travelled so I had a great ride and he made things very easy for me.

"Charlie had told me he would stay very well and he was right. It was quite emotional afterwards. It's hard to describe. I thought about my mum and dad, my family."

What of the future?

"Champion jockey is never going to happen," he says. "I'm 5 foot 11 inches, so I can't ride the lightweights. Nine stone (126 lbs) is my minimum, so to win the Derby was big. I'm not the type of guy to get a big head or anything. I just carry on. But, when I got home that evening, there were a lot of people there waiting for me and everyone seemed to have a good time. It was a great day, never to be forgotten.

I said it must have felt nice waking up the next morning. "Not really. I had a headache!"

Sadly, Maurice Kirby died suddenly eight years ago. He missed most of Adam's career, and his grandchildren. "It was very sad. He missed all of it really, my big successes, but he is always with me in my heart.

CHAPTER 37

Saratoga & the Whitney

Eric Saull, who is up with Kenny McPeek's string, spilt the beans about Skydiver – and King Fury in another Grade 1 on the card, the Saratoga Derby Turf invitational. Or did he? Can I trust him, or is he a double agent, feeding me misinformation? It's a tough call with Saull, who I knew when I was assistant with McPeek and Saull walked hots. He is a big fan of Swiss Skydiver.

My son, Jack Gilligan, who is a jockey, and I wandered around the barns again in the morning. We spoke with Sean Clancy, of the *Saratoga Special*, for a while, everyone greeted Jack. Christophe Clement said to please keep him in mind if he ever moves on from race riding.

I wanted to show Jack the horse path on the Oklahoma training track. I have told him before he could scatter my ashes there. He asked if next Tuesday worked.

I loved walking up and down the pathway with the horses in the misty dawn, the air cool on my skin, surrounded both sides by giant firs and pines. it is a timeless place.

It *was* a timeless place anyway. Now the horse walk is gone, or at least half gone. They widened the track and cut down the row of trees nearest the outside rail. A travesty in my opinion. Now I suppose my ashes will just blow straight onto the track and be ploughed into it at first break. A bit disappointing, to me at least.

It was only a question of time, but that Saturday afternoon Steve Asmussen did it. He became the winningmost Thoroughbred racehorse trainer in North American history. Maybe world history.

For a trainer, Asmussen is relatively young still. He may leave a record truly untouchable. He was young when he started. He has his father and brother helping him. The whole family seem involved, so it was good to see him at the track with his family, receiving congratulations.

I didn't want to put a damper on the day, but since I am around Asmussen's age and my son is around his son's age, the uncomfortable question left hanging in the air is: What the hell had I been doing as a trainer all those years, achieving so little when he has achieved so much.

"Asmussen has trained more than 30,000 losers, son. Your dad barely lost 500 races in his whole career. And anyway, I have a mind to start again, who knows …" He knows.

We were in the paddock later. We spoke briefly with Christophe Clement again. He asked me what I was up to now. I told him I was open to offers. He just smiled.

Maxfield must be one of the most handsome colts in the nation. He is a knockout – big, dark, imposing. I love seeing the good ones in the paddock. Maybe the good dirt horses are the most handsome of all Thoroughbreds.

Angular, powerful, brooding Maxfield walked by using his powerful stride, his neck arched, his eyes shining and liquid. The gray Knicks

Go is smaller, less imposing, at the walk at least. But he can run. Big is impressive, but it is all about power-to-weight ratio, who has the best heart and lungs relative to their size.

Swiss Skydiver, the Preakness-winning filly, a powerful chestnut, is a little washed out today, a bit fresh, her campaign has had interruptions this year, after a busy 2020. She thrived on a busy campaign last year. Maybe she is a little too fresh today, whatever she does today, she should come on for the race. *(In the event, she finished fourth of the five starters behind 4½-length winner Knicks Go. Maxfield was second.)*

After the races, everyone headed over to Fasig-Tipton. The sales company right across the street from the track was throwing a party and everyone was invited. Food and drink and live music laid on for anyone who wished to attend.

The previous day, the Hall of Fame Awards presentations took place in the Fasig Tipton Pavilion. I strolled down and was there for Mark Casse's acceptance speech (he was a 2020 inductee but there was no ceremony at the time so this was a joint 2020/21 event). His speech was funny and moving, and he was by turn laughing and crying. His owners have become his friends, and Casse seems like a fun and loyal one.

One of his owners recounted his first dealings with Casse. The owner had made a list of a bunch of fillies at the sales he was interested in. Casse took the list, looked at it, crumpled it up and threw it away. And he bought him two colts for $5,000 each.

A while later, the owner received a 7.30am call from Casse. Early morning calls from trainers are often bad-news calls. The owner answered warily.

This time Casse said those two colts had been going well and in fact someone had just offered them $60,000 for the pair. "Well maybe we should think about taking it?" The owner ventured cautiously.

"Oh, we did take it," said Casse. "I was just calling to ask you where you want the check sent."

Casse said he first visited the Hall of Fame with his father, also a trainer, in 1972 at the age of 11. He said he told his dad then that he would be in the Hall Of Fame one day. He cried when he recounted that his father replied, "Yes Mark, you will."

CHAPTER 38
Steeplechasing at the Spa

The Clancy Brothers may sound like the name of a traditional Irish music band, or even a pair of outlaws, but they are, in real life, media magnates.

Proprietors of the famed Saratoga Special, the newspaper that is published in Saratoga Springs during the race meet and which provides insightful, humorous, and sometimes poignant coverage and commentary of the whole thing that is Saratoga. It is a cherished thing, and not an inconsiderable part of the charm of summer days in Saratoga Springs.

If someone could cajole the Clancy Brothers into running this treasured publication year-round and nationally, covering only the other elite race meets of North America, then the sport would be well served.

Joe and Sean Clancy spent every summer in Saratoga as children. Their father was a racehorse trainer and they came up with him and his horses from their farm in Pennsylvania in a 6-berth horsebox and spent carefree days there.

The brothers galloped horses as youngsters, and Sean Clancy graduated, from age 18, to riding steeplechases up and down the East Coast, including at Saratoga, which is now really the only major racecourse still hosting such events.

In 1998, he won the Grade 1 New York Turf Writers Steeplechase on Hokan.

"I grew up going to the barn with Dad, to the races with Dad," he says. "My mom, my brother and sisters and I would all go up to Saratoga in the summer. One of the earliest pictures I have is of our family together, sitting on one of those green benches down close to the quarter pole at the track and Secretariat is jogging by in the background.

"Dad trained flat horses and jumpers, but mainly jumpers. He trained for Donald P Ross's Brandywine Stables, a famous and historic outfit, and then Augustin Stable for George Strawbridge for around 14 years."

Sean Clancy went on, "We'd flop in the back of the van each summer and head off at midnight and arrive early morning. When we turned onto Union Avenue, the sun would be coming up and we'd be leaning out, and man, we'd see Saratoga in all its glory. We knew it was magical, even then.

"The jumpers were stabled at the annex across the road from the Oklahoma training track when I was a kid in the 70s. It was two big barns and they were all there, Mikey Smithwick, Jonathan Sheppard, Tom Voss, Mickey Walsh, Burley Cocks, Janet Elliot …

"There were kids running around everywhere. We set up a lemonade stand. We'd cycle downtown barefoot, ride the pony around the shed row, hotwalk the odd one, head off to the races. It was magical, the people, the horses, the ambience."

I wondered how times changed from the time he looked up at the horses to when he looked down from upon them?

"Back in the day, we'd gallop on the turf on the infield at Saratoga. Everyone wanted a maiden jump winner at Saratoga. Quality horses, by superman out of wonder woman! Mrs Ogden Phipps had a string of jumpers, Paul Mellon, powerful strings. Many trainers then had both jumpers and flat horses. That's how it was.

"Steeplechasing was just part of the sport then. I rode jump races at Delaware Park, Laurel, Calder, Tampa Bay Downs, Keeneland, Churchill, Pimlico, Suffolk Downs, Rockingham Park and all the New York tracks. Now it's just Saratoga, Colonial Downs and a couple of races at Belmont."

"Jumping was huge in New York. They raced at Belmont, Aqueduct, Saratoga. I rode jump races professionally for 13 years. The first year I rode at Saratoga was 1988,.I got three rides that meet, and I couldn't believe I got that many.

"My first ride, I finished third on a massive outsider for Janet Elliot. I remember it like it was yesterday. It was a dream come true for me. I came up every year after that. I would gallop horses each summer morning for the likes of Mickey Preger, Mike Freeman, John Hertler, PG Johnson, Mike Hushion, Leo O'Brien.

"I was at college and spent my holidays here. I earned $235 a week with Mike Freeman, which was pretty good money back then.

"Saratoga used to run about two jump races a week, so you would be hoping for about 12 rides the whole meet. The New York Turf Writers Steeplechase was the highlight of the jump races at the meet. It has just been renamed the Jonathan Sheppard Steeplechase. I was a proper Grade 1 contest."

I contacted Michael Veitch, who is the historian at Saratoga's National Museum of Racing and who himself has an illustrious racing pedigree, being the grand nephew of Hall of Famer Sylvester Veitch, who trained for Mr Whitney and Mr Widener, and Sylvester Veitch's son, John, trained Alydar.

"There was racing in Saratoga before the track opened in 1864," says Michael Veitch. "In fact, in my research, I have found evidence of a hurdle race held in 1858 at a fair on the grounds of what is now the Oklahoma training track. The first hurdle race at the actual Saratoga track was held the same year the track opened [1864] so it was there from the very beginning.

"I remember as kids, we would all cycle to Nelson Avenue, and we would tell the security guard we were going to Sylvester Veitch's barn, and when we got in we would walk right across the main track into the infield and that is where we would sit and watch the hurdles races."

That's what it is really, Saratoga, ghosts of horses and horsemen. That is what memories are really, aren't they? We walk through them all the time, we feel them, ghostly horses jumping shadows. There is probably even the ghost of a small child somewhere, running around barefoot and hustling lemonade while his Dad looks on and smiles.

CHAPTER 39

Alabama Slamma!

It rained that morning. The morning of August 18, 2018. The morning of the Alabama Stakes at Saratoga. The final piece of the jigsaw fell into place, we thought. But then the rain stopped.

It was late morning. Her race wasn't due to go off until 5.40 that afternoon. In the mean time, the track would be drying out, hour by relentless hour. How it would be come race time was anyone's guess. There was $600,000 in purse money, and another million dollars or so in bloodstock value depending on the moisture level in the track that afternoon.

We were there, Kenny, Danny, me. All suited up, pacing around, waiting at the barn.

Jannette, her groom, got her ready. Kenny started looking for things for us to do, little tasks, distractions, for himself and for us. He often puts the hind rundown bandages on himself for the Grade 1s. Once that was done, I put on the bridle, he double checked it, and we were good to go. Kenny headed off to the track. The sun was shining, it had remained dry all afternoon.

We pulled the filly out, I checked her over once again, and off she headed for the mile walk to the racecourse.

Danny and I jumped in the golf buggy and shadowed her over. She was good. She was a professional. She knew what was coming. It was exciting, being part of it.

It was back in late March I first saw her. She was hairy and dry-coated then. Now she was sleek, and proud. She was big and strong and honest. I knew she would give everything she had today, she was ready. Danny was big on her. Today couldn't come around quick enough for him.

The horses circled in the holding barn. Waiting to be called across to the paddock. Danny and I exchanged nothings, our minds focused on the race.

They were called out in racecard order to walk to the racetrack. Danny was dressed sharper than a big-time rapper. He led the way. I walked by the horse's shoulder. She felt imposing. She felt focused.

We walked through, past the throng, cutting through the picnickers and bettors. The railed walkway was lined with spectators, within touching distance each side. Fans who wanted to see some of the most gifted Thoroughbred fillies of their generation. The cream of the crop. All of us sheltered under the giant green-leaved elm trees, sunlight fingering its way through here and there.

Kenny met us in the paddock. We talked more nothings. The valet brought out the saddle. She was good to tack. She was good about everything. We circled some more. The riders entered the paddock. Jose Ortiz greeted everyone. The Puerto Rican superstar, reigning champion jockey in North America.

A few words were exchanged. Kenny told him to leave her alone the first half of the race, and at the business end, if he saw a chance to save ground, to take it. "If it doesn't work out, that's on me," he said.

Jose acknowledged him, and we went to meet the filly. He was legged up, and we began the final walk out onto the track. Hundreds of fans lined the way. Some of them shouted the jockeys. Cameras followed us. I asked Jose what the track was like. "It's wet," he said.

We let her off to the pony rider, and she stepped onto the track. She was big and golden, and the tension kept building.

The bettors were queuing deep at the windows, trying to get their money on as the horses paraded. The sky was blue and bright, wisps of clouds, the green infield, the beige track, noise everywhere.

And then they loaded, and everything stopped. The crowd fell silent, for the first time you could hear every word the announcer said. We stood in the winner's circle, right by the track, near the wire, me and Danny. And the gates sprung open, and for two minutes nothing else existed.

She broke on terms with her seven competitors, but as they ran past us towards the wire for the first time, she was already getting detached, outpaced seemingly, in last place, and she just kept dropping further back.

By the time they had travelled the first furlong and a half and were hitting the first turn, she was half a dozen lengths off the second last horse. The leader was in a different county already. We hadn't expected this.

As they swung out of the turn into the backstretch, she was out of the picture, trailing hopelessly. But then the time flashed up, 22.52 seconds for the first quarter-mile, lightning fast for a mile-and-a-quarter race, too fast, even for horses of this calibre. And, as they rolled along the backstretch and hit the half mile in 46.79, I fancied she was closing fractionally.

Then, just as they started to enter the home turn, she started to roll, to pick up, and she walked past two stragglers, kicking them out of her way, and halfway around the turn she went between two more, and Jose remembered what Kenny said, and as he went through them he darted to the inside rail. He saved ground. The muddy dirt kicked into her face, but she ignored it. And then they ducked out again as they entered the stretch, and she emerged, covered in dirt, wearing her signs of battle, and Jose urged her, and she stretched, all power, and courage and honesty. Running with all her heart, for whatever reason, for us maybe, for her survival, as her ancestors had done, for millions of years. They had all run fast enough, to stay alive long enough to reproduce, so she could be here this day. The impossibility of existence.

She burst to the front. The opposition faded to nothing. There was only her, her head stretched, her powerful stride, her giant heart, reaching for the wire, the wire she didn't even know was there. She won easily, by 6½ lengths.

Danny was ecstatic, we all were. We hugged each other, there in the winner's enclosure, and laughed along with Danny as we waited for her to come back to us. We waited for the newly crowned queen, the blue blood, the granddaughter of Winning Colors, so she would accept her blanket of flowers, and receive the worship of the crowd, of her crowd now, for today.

Kenny appeared. He looked relieved, a bit shocked, hiding the adrenaline rush, being professional – he will enjoy it later though, a plan of his, months in the making. Waiting for this one day. Bam!

She came back, Jose all smiles. She was fine, blowing hard of course, but her head was up, she wasn't exhausted, wasn't spent. Still proud. We were all proud now. She came into the winner's circle, and we had our pictures taken. And she wrote herself into the record books that day, Eskimo Kisses.

CHAPTER 40

Racing in New Orleans

The sport had probably been taking place on small, informal half-mile circuits all around Louisiana, but it was the formation of the Metairie Jockey Club on the outskirts of New Orleans that really launched horseracing in the 'Pelican State' and specifically in the New Orleans area.

Metairie racecourse opened in 1838, a full 26 years before the first races would be run up at Saratoga, and the elites of New Orleans – the plantation owners and merchants – thronged there from the beginning. The grandstand was notably grand, with separate rooms and viewing areas provided for the ladies who dressed up and came to see and be seen.

Metairie Jockey Club was an exclusive one. A Mr Charles Howard, who had made his money by setting up a successful state lottery, was denied entry. Whether it was because of his lack of creole blood, or his *nouveaux riche* status, or perhaps just because he was a Republican, is unknown. He vowed he would one day buy that racecourse, close it down and build a cemetery on that track.

Metairie became renowned for its social scene, and the sport thrived there. It became famous nationwide as the track that hosted three famous contests between Louisiana's and Kentucky's best racers.

The racehorse Lexington was owned by Richard Ten Broeck, who had become a major stakeholder in Metairie racetrack and wanted to promote it by establishing a new sweepstake, the Great State Post Stakes. Although expected to be a meeting between North and South, Lexington, from Kentucky, was the northernmost based competitor that showed up.

Lecomte was by the same sire, Boston, as Lexington. Boston was a great racehorse of his day and a champion sire. His two best sons were the swiftest horses in the nation, and now the two unbeaten superstars were to meet.

Steamboats were chartered to New Orleans and ex-president Millard Fillmore was one of the judges in attendance.

Come the day, the track turned heavy and muddy, conditions Lexington reveled in but Lecomte did not, and Lexington duly won the first two of the four-mile heats, Lecomte tasting defeat for the first time.

A week later the pair were to meet again in the Jockey Club Stakes. This time Lecomte's owner secured the services of Duncan Kenner's slave rider, known as Abe.

Abe, the greatest rider in the south, was to take on the New York-born Gilpatrick, the greatest rider in the north. Under a perfect front-running ride from Abe, Lecomte gained his revenge over Lexington, the only horse ever to beat him.

The time of 7 minutes and 26 seconds broke the track record, set when the great northern mare Fashion bested the mighty Boston a generation before.

New Orleans celebrated southern hero Lecomte's victory to the extent a remote town was named after him. They spelt his name wrong though and they say that is how Lecompte, Louisiana, came to be.

Honors were even, but it was never going to end there. Each camp believed their horse was the greatest.

Richard Ten Broeck took to the newspapers, seeking a rematch. Eventually he got it.

It was April 14, 1855, the day of the most widely anticipated rematch the sport had ever known. In the first heat, a knockout blow was delivered when Lexington won. The owners of a perhaps below-par Lecomte conceded defeat before the next heat.

The Daily Picayune described the match thus:

> *"The long agony is over – the contest is ended – the race is run! The rival champions Lexington and Lecomte, who commanded the Earth to stand still, who hushed the wind and rebuked the waves, have fought the battle."*

Lexington went on to become the greatest sire of his time, a 16-time champion. Lecomte's record in the breeding shed was not as impressive, but he found success as a sire of broodmares and the relatively recent European champion fillies Sonic Lady and Attraction carried his blood.

The civil war took Metairie's good fortunes and many great southern bloodlines with it when Union soldiers raided the plantations and plundered the horses.

Abe, the slave rider, escaped to the north and won the 1866 running of the Travers at Saratoga as Abe Hawkins, then a free man.

Metairie racecourse never really recovered and was closed. The newly built Fair Grounds racecourse, just a couple of miles away in

Bayou St John, took over. Charles Howard did buy that racecourse and was later interred there himself.

There were other tracks in New Orleans that came and went. The first was the Eclipse, opened in 1837. City Park had a racetrack, and there was Jefferson Downs, but Metairie ruled it all and Fair Grounds flies the flag now.

Built in 1865, the Luling Mansion sat on 80 acres, which ran right up to Bayou St John. It was commissioned by a successful German merchant, Florenz Luling, as his family home. Not long after moving in, though, his business began to fail, and then his two sons drowned in that bayou. The designer of the mansion, famed architect James Gallier, later drowned also, when a ship he was sailing in sunk.

The German merchant sold the mansion and returned to Europe with what was left of his family. Perhaps Luling shouldn't have purchased land that ran right up to the bayou, as that was where the 'Voodoo Queen',Marie Laveau (1801-1881), liked to hold large celebrations after sundown each St Johns Eve. The Louisiana jockey Club ran the Fair Grounds track and purchased the opulent Italianite Luling Mansion right behind the racecourse as the clubhouse. It became known for the glamorous dinners and cocktail parties held there.

Fair Grounds opened its doors in 1872, but horses had raced on the same spot sporadically since Metairie's first days, making it seemingly the oldest Thoroughbred racecourse in the USA to still be operating, albeit not continuously. In 1839, there was a first brief meeting at the 'Louisiana Racetrack'. Then, in 1852, it opened again, this time as the Union Racetrack, but it fell to competition from Metairie before reopening once more in 1872, this time as Fair Grounds.

Opening day now is traditionally on Thanksgiving, and the locals dress up as for Mardi Gras and flock to the track, providing a wild, colorful spectacle unique in the racing world.

Now horses are back at Fair Grounds for this year's meet, hundreds and hundreds of them, their bloodlines noted and recorded for centuries. Next year's Kentucky Derby winner could be among them.

Two winners of the Louisiana Derby have gone on to take *The Roses*, Grindstone in 1996 and Black Gold in 1924.

Black Gold ran his last race at the Fair Grounds. He broke his ankle in the stretch and was buried in the infield. A monument stands to him there.

The French impressionist Edgar Degas visited New Orleans in the autumn of 1872 for five months. His mother's family had a grand home on a stone's throw from the newly opened Fair Grounds racecourse and the Luling Mansion, and he regularly attended both during his stay.

Although best known for his paintings of ballerinas, racehorses were another favorite subject. Someone asked him once why he returned to them so often, why he revisited those same poses again and again?

"A horse without a rider is still a horse," he replied. "But a man without a horse is just a man.

CHAPTER 41

Pan Zareta & Tippity Witchet

Although largely forgotten today, in the first half of the 20th century the names Tippity Witchet and Pan Zareta were known throughout North America.

At a time when horseracing was part of the national consciousness, these two plied their trade across the nation and beyond into Mexico and Canada and even Cuba. They ran more races and won more races than could be considered possible now.

Pan Zareta, or 'Panzy' as she was affectionately known, was foaled in Texas in 1910. The little chestnut foal was named after Pansy Zareta, the daughter of the Mayor of Juarez, who was a friend of the breeder, James F Newman.

Pan Zareta's sire, Abe Frank, means little now, and her dam, Caddie Griffith, may not stand close scrutiny either, but together they produced a filly who became known as the queen of the U.S. turf and was to be inducted into not only the Fair Grounds and Texas racing halls of fame, but the national one in Saratoga too.

Panzy became famous across the North American continent. People traveled miles to see her race. She wasn't famous because of the top races she competed in, though, because she didn't compete in the top races. In fact, many of her wins came in minor contests. She just became famous and loved for her toughness and ability to win.

She won the Señorita Stakes, the Rio Grande stakes, the Chihuahua Stakes. She won some handicaps, and she set a world record time for five furlongs at Juarez racetrack – 57.2 seconds (hopefully cheered on by Pansy, her namesake) – that stood for 31 years. She set 11 track records over the course of her career.

What Pan Zareta became most famous for was her incredible career. She ran 151 times and won 76 of them. She finished in the money 128 times in spite of having to carry up to 140lbs at times, always conceding weight to her opponents.

When she set that world record time, she was conceding 10lb to her male runner-up.

Pan Zareta beat Kentucky Derby winners Old Rosebud in one of two encounters she had with him. She raced in three countries, eight U.S. states and 24 racetracks. The traveling alone seems extraordinary, although travel by rail may have been a better experience for horses than any travel choice we can provide for them today.

Pan Zareta earned the Newman family $39,000 over the six years she competed, and in 1918 she was retired to stud. Sadly she was found to be infertile and it was elected to return her to training.

She was at Fair Grounds in New Orleans when she fell ill and developed pneumonia and died in her stall there. She was buried in the infield.

She was later to be joined there by Kentucky Derby winner Black Gold, whose dam, Useeit, she had battled on the track.

The Pan Zareta Stakes is still run each year at Fair Grounds in testament to the one-time queen of the American turf.

Tippity Witchet is an even more remarkable story of a hard-working horse. The diminutive runner almost makes Pan Zareta look like a good-for-nothing layabout.

By Travers winner and leading sire Broomstick and out of the St Simon mare Lady Frivoles, little Tippity had claims to greatness, but again his name was not made in the great stakes, although he did compete at the highest levels early in his career.

As a 2-year-old, he won 14 of his 20 starts, winning eight in one 7-week period, including the 1917 Aberdeen Handicap at Havre De Grace and was considered one of the top juveniles in the nation.

His owner sold him for $3,000 at the end of that year, and his second owner auctioned him some races later, receiving $20,000 for the little horse. He changed hands many times and was a loyal friend to all who cared for him.

Tippity Witchet raced from 2 until the age of 14. He won at 27 of the 31 racetracks he competed on. He raced in Mexico in Canada and in Cuba, he won on fast ground and in the mud, he won over six furlongs and he won over a mile and a half, he won multiple stakes and numerous claimers, often changing hands, and he kept racing and he kept winning.

At the age of 12 he won 12 races.

In 1928 the Washington Post wrote, "Perhaps no horse more deserves the title of selling plater king of the American turf than Tippity Witchet."

The following year he sustained an injury in a race and was retired. He earned his retirement.

Pony-sized Tippity Witchet took part in 266 races in his 12-year career. He was 14 when he ran the last one. He emerged victorious in 78 of those contests, was in the money 172 times and earned over $88,000 for his connections. He spent a large portion of his career competing at Fair Grounds and was inducted into the hall of fame there.

There were calls for this horse, famous across America in his day, to be inducted into the national hall of fame despite his modest status. The king of the selling platers is not inducted yet.

After his retirement in 1929, he remained in active service as a pony at trainer Lionel Bauer's stable. It was thought being idle would be against Tippity's nature.

Two remarkable Thoroughbreds, two examples of great service horses have provided to people for millennia. All they have asked for in return is to be cared for and respected.

Here is the kicker though. Tippity Witchet's race record is scarcely believable to modern eyes, it is hard to imagine any Thoroughbred could ever come close to such a feat, to race so many time and for so long. For one horse to rack up 78 wins is incredible.

However, the splendidly named, small, but giant hearted Tippity Witchet is only the fourth winning-most racehorse to compete in North America – behind three horses from the 1800s – Kingston (by Spendthrift) with 89 wins, Bankrupt (also by Spendthrift) with 86 and Catherina (by Whisker) with 79.

CHAPTER 42

Jimmy Winkfield

In 1882 eight miles east of Lexington Kentucky in a town called Uttinger, was born Jimmy Winkfield, the seventeenth child of seventeen children.

Young Winkfield grew up enthralled by the Thoroughbreds training and racing at the nearby Kentucky Association Racetrack and he vowed that one day he would become a jockey.

He did become a jockey, he became a great great jockey, he became much in demand and he rode as far north as Roby Indiana, where he said the wind from lake Michigan would freeze the reins to his hands and he rode as far south as The Fair Grounds in New Orleans.

There was a race war beginning though, the white riders coveted the black riders mounts and rough rode them in races, which started to make owners and trainers reluctant to use black riders less their horses were fouled.

In spite of that Jimmy Winkfield won back to back Kentucky Derbies, in 1901 & 1902. The first rider to do so since the celebrated

Isaac Murphy who was widely considered the best rider ever at that time to have pulled on the silks.

You would have thought that enough excitement, enough achievement for one black man, or for a white one for that matter to win two Kentucky Derbies in those days. But James Winkfield was just getting going.

By 1903 due to the race wars, and in part due to spinning a big owner who threatened afterwards to ruin him, Winkfield found himself heading to Russia of all places to ride under contract.

American riders were prized in Europe then and Winkfield found his color to be no barrier in Tsarist Russia, and by the end of 1904 he was leading rider. The Russian aristocracy rewarded jockeys generously, so much so that Winkfield took a suite in Moscow's finest hotel and dressed in the finest clothes put out for him by his private valet, and liked to breakfast on caviar – the rewards for winning the Moscow, Warsaw and St Petersburg derbies that year, a feat never accomplished before. James Winkfield liked winning Derbies.

Winkfield returned to the States that winter to holiday and found that nearly every black rider was gone from the ranks, and increasingly from the horse farms also, being pushed out of the sport, a better life was hoped to be found in factories and most of the black horsemanship passed down from generation to generation for over two hundred years was suddenly all but gone. And, for a long time after, the memories of those horsemen disappeared and was forgotten also.

Winkfield returned to Russia, continued to be a great success. He was also tempted by a Polish prince and a German baron to ride in Austria and Germany for them.

With the start of the Russian Revolution 1917 however, came change. The far-left Bolsheviks were dismantling the great wealth and power the Monarchy and aristocracy possessed – and they, of course, were the owners of the racehorses.

Winkfield decided it was time to resume his travels and so he and a party of racetrackers headed off to safety – with 200 racehorses in tow.

It was a thousand mile trek, they were shot at, chased from villages, some horses starved to death, some were eaten, but two months later they arrived in Warsaw, and from there Winkfield headed to Paris to reunite with old connections.

In Paris Winkfield's career took off again, he met and married an exiled Russian aristocrats daughter, and they set up home and a stables in Maison-Laffitte on the city's outskirts.

A decade later, in 1930, at the age of 48 Jimmy Winkfield hung up his racing boots and retired after notching over 2,500 wins in eight different countries.

As a trainer, again Winkfield found success and was now settled with his son and daughter and wife. But then the German army rolled into town, and Winkfield, together with his family, rolled out and made passage to the States.

With most of his wealth left behind, Winkfield worked as a stable hand, eventually got to train a few, tried to help a couple of black apprentices get going as riders, but he said they never got to first base.

It was 1953 before Winkfield returned to France, he and his son started training together at their same home.

Winkfield returned to America in 1960, he required an operation, and, convinced that he would not survive it, said he wanted to have it in Kentucky, so he could be buried there.

To his great embarrassment the operation was a success, so he went and stayed afterwards with his daughter, now the wife of a surgeon in Cincinnati, and the following year he decided to go see the 1961 run for the roses.

It had been fifty-eight years since "Winkfield, the Great Jockey," had last ridden in the Kentucky, since he last was at Churchill Downs.

Afterwards the Turf Writers Association held a banquet for the now 78 year old man at the famous Brown Hotel in Louisville, he had been away a long time now though. When he and his daughter tried to enter the hotel they were told they needed to use another entrance.

Eventually guests from the banquet persuaded management to let him in, but once sat he was nearly completely ignored his daughter recounted bitterly years later. It was their loss, the stories he could have told them.

Jimmy Winkfield returned to France, to his home, where he died in 1974 at the age of ninety-one. The rider who won back to back Derbies at the very dawn of the 1900's, was the last of the great black jockeys.

In 2004 Jimmy Winkfield was inducted into the US Horse Racing National Hall Of Fame. Embraced at last by the country he had always loved.

CHAPTER 43

Sir Mark Prescott Part Two

He was stood behind the front door, Jack, fixing me with his eyes. We had seen William Butler walking toward our house through our living room window. We both headed toward that door for different reasons.

Willam told me how much everyone at Heath House had loved having Jack with them for a month's work experience and would he be interested in joining them as their apprentice when he shortly finished school. Jack, stood behind the door started shaking his head furiously. "He'd love to I said."

Every morning he would head off to Heath House an exhausted wreck, like an overworked underfed urchin heading for the workhouse, which in a way, I suppose, he was. But the thing is every day at around 11am he would return full of stories, laughing to his belly and recounting the morning's adventures.

He was taught so much at Heath House, horsemanship of course, but punctuality, tidiness, manners, respect, consistency, hard work. He still has those values he picked up from Sir Mark.

Sir Mark and I were neighbours for sixteen years. The first morning I encountered him I said good morning Sir Mark and he replied good morning Mr Gilligan. On my last morning in Newmarket, before we left for the States, I said good morning Sir Mark and he replied, good morning, Mr Gilligan.

I knew of him, from years earlier though, I would read of his exploits sat at the back of the bus with the Sporting Life on my way to school. A "job" team Prescott and Duffield, my Irish Stepfather would tell me. He never told me about algebra, but he told me about "Prescott and Duffield."

Jack worked the mandatory year before his first ride for Sir Mark. A Lingfield Park evening meeting and Sir Mark in attendance! Even the television presenters commented on it. I think the nag was supposed to win, I think Sir Mark was going to say something nice about Jack afterwards. I shall always believe that even if it were not true. They finished second in the end but I know Sir Mark grew to like and have respect for Jack as the whole team at Heath House seemingly did and I have liked them in return ever since, for that.

So, when word came to the New World that the gallant Alpinista had won the Prix de l'Arc de Triomphe a smile came across my face. I called Jack later, he told me it was the most happy he had ever been to see someone else win.

I asked him if they had interviewed Prescott. He said they did, he said that Prescott was emotional, that it choked him up a bit watching him. Then I choked up a bit too.

Make the most of him. There won't be another one of him, ever. The world has changed too much, society has changed too much. Everything has changed too much. That is why the seeming unchanging nature of Sir Mark and Heath House is cherished so much.

Sir Henry Cecil and Sir Mark. I thought I would be pleased to leave the class system of Britain behind, but those were the two trainers who left me always tongue tied on the heath.

He has loved that heath, Sir Mark, it is well known. The eternal Heath. I hope one day he haunts it, as Fred Archer is reputed to. Maybe they will meet sometime and talk together one moonlit night, and speak of ghostly gambles.

Luke Morris rode his first ever winner for me, on a little filly called Caerphilly Gal. It was a lowly banded race at Southwell. I bet though, still, that little fish tasted sweet to him then all those years ago.

Now he has won maybe the greatest horserace in the world. I bet the studious serious young boy was dreaming even then though. The thing about Luke is he doesn't just seem to remember everything about every horse he has ridden, he seems to remember everything about every horse everyone else has ridden also.

And to William Butler? Of course all congratulations to the most vital cog in the team. But thank you also, for coming and finding Jack that day.

Kirsten Rausing gave Sir Mark his greatest winner. Maybe more than that though, she made sure he was there to savour it, to breathe in the Paris air that autumn afternoon.

Jack says now, looking back, that some of his happiest memories are of his days at Heath House. And what are we left with in the end after all, except for memories made.

To Conclude

So, that is what I have to offer, If you reached this far then I hope you enjoyed some of the stories of horses and people and places.

I have enjoyed my time writing, I only really started in earnest when I was fifty after a lifetime riding and training racehorses. I wrote two books in that time and around eighty articles for various horse racing publications. I found the research enjoyable and the writing often meditative, perhaps in some part because of my age.

I have had horses in my life since the age of eleven, I think I have found comfort in them. My father passed away when I was young, perhaps that affected me in some way. Whatever the reason my own family were convinced I was crazy throughout my life really, but when I was working around horses I found solace there. I found that an early morning gallop really was the cure for all ills.

I haven't galloped a horse since I arrived in The States nine years ago. Perhaps that is what I have been missing, because now everyone in the States who knows of me is convinced I am crazy also.

I am not crazy – a little frayed probably. But if you aren't a little frayed by my age then you probably haven't gone at it hard enough. I may be touched a little by madness, but sometimes now I look around me and wonder if maybe I was one of the few sane ones.

I hope anyway that my writing has conveyed some feelings and emotions that I have often in my life been unable to articulate or speak out loud. I hope my writing has evoked in some, more tender feelings than I evoke in people so often in real life.

After 57 years on this beautiful planet I finally found the reason I think for life the universe and everything, and it isn't 42.

It is love of course, and I hope I have written with some love because I have sometimes found it a difficult thing to express in my actual life and that has brought me great sorrow at times.

And on that note I'll leave you now and probably go and hug a tree somewhere.

Gladiators, I salute you!

www.ingramcontent.com/pod-product-compliance
Lightning Source LLC
Chambersburg PA
CBHW060557310726
48982CB00008B/1154/J

* 9 7 8 1 7 3 2 8 8 9 2 8 6 *